The

Angel
Experience

The
Angel
Experience

Your complete angel workshop in a book

Hazel Raven

A GODSFIELD BOOK
www.godsfield.co.uk

An Hachette UK Company
www.hachette.co.uk

First published in Great Britain in 2010 by
Godsfield, a division of Octopus Publishing Group Ltd
Endeavour House
189 Shaftesbury Avenue
London
WC2H 8JY
www.octopusbooksusa.com

Distributed in the U.S. and Canada by Octopus Books USA:
c/o Hachette Book Group
237 Park Avenue
New York, NY 10017

ISBN 978-1-84181-393-6

Printed and bound in China

2 4 6 8 10 9 7 5 3 1

CONTENTS

Introduction 8
How to use the book and CD 12
Recording your insights 14
Glossary of terms 16

What are angels? 17
The angel hierarchies 18
Angels and spirit guides 20
The nine ranks of angelic beings 22
Principal angels 28
The elemental kingdom 32
Exercises to focus on angels 33
EXERCISE 1: Relaxation 34
EXERCISE 2: Exploring angel energies 38
EXERCISE 3: Angels of the spheres awareness 42
EXERCISE 4: Archangels meditation 46

Connecting with angels 49
Angels and chakras 50
Crystals and the angels 58
Exercises to connect with angels 65
EXERCISE 5: Chakra awareness visualization 66
EXERCISE 6: Activating your angelic chakra 70
EXERCISE 7: Angelic crystal meditation 74
EXERCISE 8: Angelic alignment using a crystal 78

Welcoming angels 81
Angel visions 82
Creating an angel altar 84
The Kabala 86
Creating an angel prayer 88
Sound and angels 90
Angelic mantras 92
Temples of light 94
Exercises to welcome angels 97
EXERCISE 9: Your angel vision 98
EXERCISE 10: Angel altar blessing 100
EXERCISE 11: Tree of Life meditation 102
EXERCISE 12: Sound meditation 106
EXERCISE 13: Angel temple meditation 108

Guardian angels 113
Your guardian angel 114
Your guiding angels 116
Guardian angels in history 118
Stories of guardian angels 120
Planetary angels 122
Qualities of the planets 124
Your personal zodiac angel 126
Exercises to attract guardian angels 129
EXERCISE 14: Journey to meet your guardian angel 130
EXERCISE 15: Guardian-angel collage 134
EXERCISE 16: Celtic angel meditation 138
EXERCISE 17: Finding your zodiac angel 140

Angel healing 145

How angels can heal 146
Physical healing 148
Emotional healing 150
Spiritual healing 152
Distant healing 154
Dream healing 156
Guidance 158
Relationships 160
Exercises for angel healing 161
EXERCISE 18: Healing meditation 162
EXERCISE 19: Loving meditation 164
EXERCISE 20: Spiritual growth meditation 168
EXERCISE 21: Planetary healing meditation 172
EXERCISE 22: Incubating a healing dream 175

Angels of assistance 177

Angelic intervention 178
Assistance in times of weakness 180
Emotional assistance 182
Assistance in finding your destiny 184
Assistance in clairvoyance 186
Finding other Earth angels 188
Angelic humans 190
Angel letters 192
Exercises to summon angel assistance 193
EXERCISE 23: Angel affirmation 194
EXFRCISE 24: Ritual for promoting spiritual growth 196
EXERCISE 25: Meditation for angelic assistance 200
EXERCISE 26: In times of trouble meditation 204
EXERCISE 27: Earth angels group meditation 207

Taking angel work further 209
Developing wisdom 210
Inspiration 212
Protection and cutting ties 214
Spiritual growth 216
Finding love 218
Assistance on your life path 220
Divination 222
Angel cards 224
Exercises to take angel work further 225
EXERCISE 28: Asking for wisdom meditation 226
EXERCISE 29: Asking for guidance meditation 230
EXERCISE 30: Asking for protection meditation 234
EXERCISE 31: Asking for renewed energy meditation 238
EXERCISE 32: Cloud divination 241

Real-life experiences 243
An angelic vision 244
The spirit of obsidian 245
Angelic signature 246
Sacred sound 247
Angel attunement 248
Angels' blessing 249
Web of light 250
A sign from a guardian angel 251

Index 252
Acknowledgments 256

CD tracks
TRACK 1: Relaxation
TRACK 2: Activating your angelic chakra
TRACK 3: Angelic alignment using a crystal
TRACK 4: Angel altar blessing
TRACK 5: Journey to meet your guardian angel
TRACK 6: Finding your zodiac angel
TRACK 7: Loving meditation

Introduction

My book *The Angel Bible* describes the attributes of many of the most well-known and beloved archangels and angels. I am now taking you further than ever before, because I am about to show you how to experience the angelic realm of love, light, and healing for yourself, with the help of this book and its accompanying CD. You will open your mind and heart to the celestial worlds as we experience together the exciting, life-changing, and often heart-warming energies of the angels.

If you are new to the angelic realm, you will feel comfortable here. And if you are an experienced angel enthusiast, you may find renewed inspiration.

Whether you are a beginner or have been exploring the angelic kingdom for some time, this book and CD provide a personalized, practical, direct experience of the profound wisdom that can be yours when you connect with your angels. Going far beyond a reference guide, this book is more like a personal tutor, leading you through key ideas and concepts via inspirational and practical, holistic, hands-on exercises. It is like attending an angel seminar with me, in which I show you how to experience the angels at first hand.

I have consciously worked with several specific archangels—vast, powerful beings that help us and oversee the guardian angels—and I have presented information about them at my many workshops. During my angel readings and therapy sessions I frequently help people to understand which angels are with them. In fact, during my readings I meet many angels that are new to me. Sometimes I ask a seminar delegate if he or she knows there is a multitude of angels around him or her.

I have never felt comfortable telling people which angels they "should" talk to. Although I work closely with the archangels Gabriel and Michael, I do not feel compelled to push them on others. My role is to assist and encourage people. I tell them of the uniqueness of each being, and that everyone is different and every angelic experience is personal. We are all the product of our upbringing, past conditioning, spiritual practices, and life experiences. In my workshops I teach people how to release their emotional blocks by opening the channels of Divine communication, so that they can more clearly see, hear, feel, and know these beautiful celestial beings.

This book is an introduction, a gateway to the celestial realms of love, light, healing, and inspiration. I recommend that you create your own journal—your angel directory—so that as you work with each angel you can record whether you feel happier, healthier, more inspired and balanced or more relaxed and peaceful when you connect to them.

Over the many years in which I have been running angel workshops I have helped thousands of people awaken to the angelic realm. Allow me to be your guide and mentor as we discover some of the exciting possibilities that the angels have to offer, helping you not only to relax, but also improve your ability to visualize, meditate, and hone your intuition. We will explore these subtle energies, and journey deep into your own heart and into that of the universe, as you open your inner wisdom to the ancient secrets of the celestial realms.

The symbols in this book

 Work with your angel/s now This symbol guides you to the relevant practical exercise when you are ready, where you will find full instructions to follow.

 I'm not quite there yet If you don't yet feel confident about doing the exercise, this symbol gives suggestions for ways to revise and prepare yourself.

 Work with the CD now This symbol tells you when you need to turn on the CD and which track to select.

How to use the book and CD

This book is a complete and personalized program that is suitable both for beginners and for those who have a greater understanding of angels. Each section of the book explains specific areas of angel wisdom that will expand your knowledge and help you work more closely with the celestial realms.

As you will discover, each section is divided into two parts. The first part gives you the information that you need about a particular area of the angel kingdom, before you embark on the second part, in which you are shown how to connect with that area yourself. There is no time limit and there are no rules, so you are free to take these sections at your own pace. You can repeat a section as many times as you wish until you feel ready to move on to the next section.

The second part of each section is designed to help you link directly with the angels through a series of exercises

and rituals. There are spaces where you can write down your experiences, going into detail about the information and inspiration that you have received.

As you work with this book, remember that your main teachers are the angels themselves as they guide you to gain more knowledge, experience, and confidence. The angels await your summons!

The CD is intended to put you into the best possible state of mind for connecting with the angels. When you play the track recommended for an exercise (as directed by the CD symbol) you will be given the relevant instructions and then you will hear a piece of music that is designed to help you carry them out. You will then be taken on to the next stage. If you need more time for a particular exercise, you can pause the CD and/or follow the "I'm not there yet" suggestions, which offer ways to revise and prepare yourself.

Recording your insights

As you work your way through this book, a picture will emerge of your own insights and experiences. If you are to get the most out of this course you need to create your own personal evaluation journal. This is a record of achievement that is exclusive to you. It illustrates how you have arrived at this point on your angelic journey, by charting the progress you make on each section of the course. Personal experiences can dissipate like a dream unless they are written down.

Varying the time at which you do the exercises is important, for it helps you establish whether there is a particular period of the day when you are more intuitive and receptive to the angels. Do not be overly concerned if you cannot fully understand the experience right away; fragmentary information often occurs in subsequent meditations. Some experiences may make no sense to you for weeks, months, or even years, so your journal will become a special way of assimilating knowledge and wisdom.

Don't be concerned about your spelling or writing style; allow yourself literary freedom. Try to record your experiences in the present tense—"I am walking... I am entering..." and so on—because this helps you to enter more fully into the experience. It is essential that you record as much information as possible, however vague, fragmented, or nebulous it may seem to you. Always pay attention to your body, especially the sensations you feel, including the thoughts that flow through your mind, the sounds that you become aware of, your breathing, your heartbeat, and the atmosphere in the room.

The journal entries include questions to help you focus on how the angel in question affected you, the emotional or energetic changes it brought about, and the insights you have received. Filling these in as fully as possible will assist you in gaining a deeper knowledge of the angelic realm. Don't hesitate to go back and add to your record if you suddenly remember something else—put the date and time beside it, so that you know this is an addition to the original record. After each meditation give yourself time to assimilate what you have learned.

Glossary of terms

Angelology
The study of angels.

Archangel
One of the vast, powerful beings that control everything in God's creation (and oversee the guardian angels), thereby bringing harmony and peace.

Aura
A bio-magnetic energy field that surrounds all living creatures.

Celestial hierarchy
Different rankings of angelic beings, commonly believed to consist of nine ranks divided into three spheres.

Chakra
A subtle-energy center located along the spine of the body; according to both Hindus and Buddhists, there are seven main chakras in the body: the crown, third-eye, throat, heart, solar-plexus, sacral, and root chakras; plus the angelic and soul-star chakras.

The etheric (realm)
One of the higher planes of existence.

Guardian angel
An angel who protects and guides you through life.

Legions of light
The angels (the Virtues) and humans that the Archangel Michael enlists to provide spiritual teachings or acts of protection.

Light-worker
Someone who is aware of their own higher spiritual purpose and tries to act accordingly.

Mantra
A sacred sound, syllable, word, or group of words, repeated many times to clear negativity or to connect with enlightened consciousness.

Subtle energy
The energy field that surrounds the human body.

Temple of light
Also known as an angelic ashram, this is the temple of an archangel that is "anchored" in the etheric.

WHAT ARE ANGELS?

The angel hierarchies

Angels connect us with God. They act as intermediaries between Heaven and Earth and are pure channels of Divine love. They are eternally connected with the bliss of God's love, and work with each of us so that we can have a better understanding of that love. The word "angel" comes from the ancient Greek *angelos*, meaning "messenger."

There are countless angels, each performing a specific function. We tend to think of them as male or female because that is what we are used to on Earth, but in fact their male and female qualities are perfect and they are therefore androgynous—of indeterminate sex. Many people believe that all the angels were created by God simultaneously on the second day of creation. Each angel was perfect and immortal, and each one was given the gift of free will. Nevertheless, most angels immediately surrendered their free will and chose to devote themselves to God. A few angels, however, preferred to retain their own power, and these are known as "fallen" angels. Those angels who renounced their free will are believed to protect humanity from these "fallen" angels.

Angels belong to pure spirit and have to obey cosmic law. Unlike humans, they are unconstrained by the limitations of time and space, which is why they are able to perform so many miraculous acts. They appear to us in numerous different forms, but perhaps the most intense and moving experiences occur when they show themselves in all their winged, celestial glory.

Islam, Christianity, and Judaism agree that the angels inhabit seven heavens and that they are arranged in a hierarchy. However, this does not mean that some angels are more important than others. Each one is special.

> **Work with your angels now** Turn to Exercise 1: Relaxation on pages 34–35, CD track 1, to get you into a relaxed state, ready to begin accessing angel power.

Angels and spirit guides

Angels are all around us, but often we cannot see them. Perhaps it is because we do not expect to encounter them. However, once we are able to open our minds and hearts to receive them, we find that they are immediately with us. Indeed, angels are increasingly making their presence felt—not only to prophets and visionaries, but to many other people besides—in numbers that are too vast to count. Many souls are awakening to the love and wisdom of the angels as they ignite the Divine spark that dwells in each person's heart.

What does an angel look like? Although the traditional image is of a glorious creature with exquisite wings, beautiful robes, and a golden halo, angels appear in many different forms. Some materialize exactly when we need them and may even seem to be ordinary humans, except that when we look again they have vanished in a way that no human ever could.

There is an infinite number of angels, each performing a specific task. We may never encounter most of them, yet each of us has a guardian angel that was assigned to us from the moment we incarnated. This angel acts as our protector and helper throughout our life, whether or not we know of our guardian angel's existence. Yours is beside you right now, as you read these words. Are you ready to strengthen your relationship with this angel, with the help of this book?

Whether or not you already work with angels, this book and its accompanying CD are intended to inspire, nourish, and awaken your heart center. Once you are awakened, you will never feel alone because you will know there is always an angel by your side.

 **Work with your angels now** To begin meditating on the angels surrounding you, turn to Exercise 2: Exploring Angel Energies on page 38.

The nine ranks of angelic beings

Angels are generally believed to be divided into nine different ranks or choirs. Each of these ranks belongs to a particular level or sphere of angelic influence.

Sphere one

This is the realm of the three highest ranks of angels—the Seraphim, Cherubim, and Thrones. Of all the angels, these are the closest to God. When we journey through this transcendent space we become surrounded by multicolored spheres of light that sound harmonious tones.

Seraphim According to Jewish law, Seraphim are the highest order of angels and therefore have the honor of surrounding God's throne. They are associated with Divine fire, light, and love. After God, they are the most light-filled beings in creation, and they have the power to purify us with flashes of lightning and cleansing flames. The word Seraphim means "the inflamer" and derives from the Hebrew word *Saraph*, which means "burning." Seraphim have six wings and continually sing God's praises with the *Trisagion*, which translates as "Holy, Holy, Holy." This sphere is ruled by the archangels Michael, Seraphiel, and Metatron.

Cherubim This is the second-highest order of angels. Cherubim were first described by either the Assyrians or the Akkadians, with the Akkadian word *karibu* meaning "one who prays." They were depicted in ancient Assyrian, Babylonian, and Chaldean art. Although Cherubim have often been painted by Western artists as chubby, Cupid-like creatures, in fact they are vast, cosmic angels that contain the energy of the sun, moon, and stars. Cherubim are ruled by the archangels Gabriel and Raphael.

Thrones These angels are always in the presence of God and are said to include the Virgin Mary. Ezekiel in the Old Testament wrote of them as a whirlwind, with their wings joined together to form huge fiery wheels full of eyes. Thrones are the wheels of Merkavah, which is God's chariot throne. They are ruled by the archangels Jophiel, Raziel, Tzaphkiel, and Zadkiel.

Sphere two

The Dominations, Virtues, and Powers, which collectively form the second-highest rank of angels, dwell in the second sphere.

Dominations Also known as the Lords, Lordships, or Dominions, these angels oversee the lower angelic hierarchy. In addition, they channel God's love and majesty through the energy of mercy, and use their powers with wisdom and compassion. They control the area where the spiritual and physical levels meet. Each Domination holds a golden staff in its right hand and a scepter, or orb, in its left hand. These angels are ruled by the archangels Muriel, Yahariel, and Zadkiel.

Virtues These angels are also known as the "shining" or "brilliant" ones, and their work is to give courage and grace to all human beings who need help. Indeed, it is the Virtues that inspire the saints. It is said that when Jesus ascended into Heaven he was escorted by two Virtues. When Eve gave birth to Cain, the Virtues acted as her midwives. These angels are ruled by the archangels Cassiel, Gabriel, and Uriel.

Powers The powers are also known as the potentates and authorities and, as their names suggest, these angels perform a very important task. They protect the souls of all human beings and are also the keepers of the Akashic Records. These records exist far beyond the boundaries of space and time, and contain every scrap of information about the past, present, and future. Another vital task of the Powers is to act as guardians over the pathways to Heaven and to prevent demons taking over the world. In addition, they are often said to be the angels of death and rebirth. These angels are ruled by the archangels Camael, Chamuel, Ertosi, Sammael, and Verchiel.

Sphere three

The Principalities, archangels, and angels dwell in this third sphere.

Principalities As you might guess from their name, these angels are responsible for the protection of nations, as well as smaller groups of people, including towns, cities, and villages. Some of the Principalities may be the guardians of more than one country: for instance, Archangel Michael is said to watch over Israel as well as Spain and other countries. In addition they help to steer religions, and their leaders, toward the truth, and they work with everyone's guardian angels. These angels are ruled by Anael, Cerviel, Haniel, and Requel.

Archangels These are the angels whose names are usually most familiar to us. The Book of Enoch, which was omitted from the Bible but contains a great deal of information about angels, lists the seven archangels as Gabriel, Haniel, Michael,

Raguel, Raphael, Seraquel, and Uriel. However, other ancient writings name different angels. Enoch described the angels as being alike, with shining faces and dressed in identical robes, standing before the throne of God. Although they are seven angels, they also make up one composite being. Perhaps for this reason they operate on many different levels simultaneously, in their role as Divine messengers who bear God's decrees.

Angels This order includes the guardian angels, whose task is to keep a watchful eye over each member of the human race. Indeed, everything in creation is under the guidance of a specific angel and, as a result, there are countless millions of angels in this order. They bring many positive gifts, including beauty, harmony, peace, joy, courage, and love, into our lives. The Old and New Testaments contain many references to angels, although they are not always identified.

Work with your angels now To work with the angels of the spheres, turn to Exercise 3: Angels of the Spheres Awareness on pages 42–43.

I'm not quite there yet If you don't feel comfortable with the angels of the spheres return to Exercise 1: Relaxation (pages 34–35) and Exercise 2: Exploring Angel Energies (page 38) to attune yourself to the angelic realm.

Principal angels

There are many angels you can call on for help and healing. You will find a complete guide in *The Angel Bible*. Below is a quick summary of 20 powerful and loving archangels.

Archangel Raphael Raphael is a powerful angel of healing; in fact his name means "God has healed" and it is his task to help those in need of medical help. Raphael can help you both heal yourself and heal others. He is the chief of the guardian angels. He is often shown carrying the caduceus—the staff symbolizing healing.

Archangel Ariel Ariel's name means "Lion of God" and his powerful energy is like the fire of the sun. He can support general health and vitality and is particularly helpful when you or your loved ones need re-energizing and transforming the negative to the joyful and positive.

Archangel Sabrael Sabrael is particularly associated with healing diseases caused by viruses and parasites. Together with Raphael, Sabrael restores equilibrium and calm.

Archangel Thuriel Thuriel is a powerful healing angel for animals; his name means "Angel of the animals." Thuriel brings about harmony between humans and nature and is a wonderful angel to call upon to bring you closer to the natural world.

Archangel Sandalphon Sandalphon carries the prayers of humans to God and he is particularly responsible for the welfare of mankind. He protects unborn children and can help distance healing and group healing.

Archangel Chamuel Chamuel's name means "He who sees God" and he can help to heal relationships and offers protection from cruelty or jealousy.

Archangel Muriel Muriel can help heal emotional turmoil and embodies sensitive, loving, and supportive energy. Her name means "Angel of the sea."

Archangel Jophiel Jophiel's name means "Beauty of God" and he promotes wisdom, clarity, and confidence. He can help with problem-solving and insight.

Archangel Haniel Haniel can help you overcome emotional turmoil and will assist you in your soul's mission. As a warrior angel he can give you strength and encouragement when you feel weak or uncertain. His name mean's "Glory (or Grace) of God."

Archangel Michael Michael's name means "Who is as God" or "Who can stand against God." He is a powerful protector and commander-in-chief of all the angels. He can release fears and phobias and strengthen your faith.

Archangel Auriel Auriel is often known as the Angel of Destiny who can help reveal your path through life. Associated with the moon, Auriel can help you access your deep subconscious. Her name means "Light of God."

Archangel Camael Camael or Chamuel can help you overcome anger and aggression and as a warrior angel provides justice and retribution. His name means "He who sees God."

Archangel Seraphiel Seraphiel's name means "Inflamer of God." He is sometimes called the Prince of Peace and he can help to awaken your true

angelic nature. He can clear karmic imprints that can be holding you back in your current life.

Archangel Tzaphkiel Tzaphkiel can help you in the contemplation of the Divine; in fact her name means "Knowledge of God." She can help you find inner peace and deep understanding.

Archangel Uriel Uriel is a powerful angel who can guide humanity as reflected in his name, which means "Fire of God" or "Light of God." He is known as the Angel of Peace because he can resolve problems and restore harmony.

Archangel Gabriel Gabriel's name means "God is my strength" and he can offer guidance and spiritual awakening. He can light your way through life-changing experiences and cleanse and purify.

Archangel Zadkiel Zadkiel teaches us to trust in God and can help bring about self-transformation and spiritual growth. His name means "Righteousness of God."

Archangel Melchizedek His name means "King of peace and righteousness" and he can help you grow along your journey through life.

Archangel Raziel Raziel can help you explore mysteries of other dimensions in time and space. His name means "Secret of God" and he can help you develop powers of clairvoyance.

Archangel Metatron His name means "Angel of the Presence" and he can help you achieve ascension to the highest spiritual states of awareness and bliss.

 Work with your angels now To help you connect with the archangels, turn to Exercise 4: Archangels Meditation on page 46.

The elemental kingdom

Nature spirits, which rule the four elements, are the children of the angels. These spirits usually manifest as swirling mists or colored lights.

Earth Fairies and other Earth spirits rule over trees and plants, as well as the crystal and mineral kingdoms. Find a tree whose energy feels comfortable and ask if you can work with its spirit essence.

Water Mermaids and undines look after our water, as well as all the creatures that live in it. They teach us to cleanse and purify our emotions, and to adapt to the situations in which we find ourselves.

Fire Salamanders are fire spirits who guard the secrets of transformational fire energy, which ignites our Divine fire to awaken our spirit.

Air Sylphs are the air spirits who carry our prayers to the angels. When we work with sylphs we increase our mental abilities, including our imagination, intuition, communication skills, and powers of inspiration.

Devas These spirits are more evolved than the other elementals. They are the guardians of sacred sites and ancient groves.

EXERCISES TO FOCUS ON ANGELS

The following exercises will help you begin to connect
with the angelic realm.

Relaxation

Relaxation is important. If you are like most people, your body carries tension and stress, so you need to learn to relax and "open" your mind's eye—this is a vital first step before undertaking any of the journeys in this book. With practice, this whole process will take just a few moments.

Ground yourself when sitting in a chair by placing your feet flat on the floor; then visualize strong roots growing out of the soles of your feet, anchoring you firmly to the Earth. If you are sitting in a classic meditation (lotus) posture, imagine roots growing out of the base of your spine deep into Mother Earth.

Crystals and angels work together in perfect harmony. Crystals give you a tangible item to hold that can enable you to feel more empowered to connect with the angelic realm or with specific angels. If you wish to connect with the angelic realm through the assistance of crystals, you can use the gemstone known as celestite (see pages 58–60) to start with.

 ## Exercise 1 RELAXATION
CD REFERENCE TRACK 1

- **Begin by seating yourself comfortably.** Make sure you will not be disturbed.

- **Listen to the sound of my voice** and give yourself permission to relax, releasing any tension in your shoulders, neck, hands, knees, feet, and at the base of your spine.

- **Forget about the past, present, or future.** Focus on this moment and begin to be aware of your normal breathing patterns.

- **Let your awareness of your breathing expand effortlessly.** In the middle of your breathing, experience your heartbeat.

- **Allow your awareness to expand** to encompass the whole of your body.

- **Let your eyes gently close.** Consciously relax every muscle in your body, starting with your toes. When you reach the crown of your head, stay in this relaxing energy for several moments as you let your aura expand to fill the space around you. Your body is now completely relaxed, but your mind is alert and focused.

- **Now gently turn your attention to your third-eye chakra.** This is the most important center to awaken and is located between and slightly above your eyebrows. Without opening your eyes, tap the ring finger of your right hand nine times gently on the third-eye chakra: tap, tap, tap...

- **See your inner mind's eye opening** as you become conscious of this space. Your intuition is expanding as you become aware of a screen in front of you.

- **Remind yourself to stay relaxed and receptive.** With each subsequent meditation, visualization, or journey that you will undertake in the future, your intuition and inner vision will effortlessly expand and grow.

- **Seal and protect yourself at the end** as you close this relaxation exercise, by placing the palm of your left hand gently over your forehead.

- **Bring your awareness back to your surroundings** as you finish your relaxation session. Allow yourself to come back slowly, taking your time, then gently ground yourself.

- **Write down what you experienced** in the space overleaf.

My relaxation experience

Date _____ **Time** _____

I saw _____
_____
_____
_____
_____
_____
_____

I felt _____
_____
_____
_____
_____
_____

I learned _____
_____
_____
_____
_____
_____
_____

My relaxation experience

Date _____ Time _____

I saw _____

_____

_____

_____

_____

_____

I felt _____

_____

_____

_____

_____

_____

I learned _____

_____

_____

_____

_____

_____

Angel energies

Angels often have messages for us. It is up to you to develop your own sensitivity and responsiveness. In this exercise you explore angel energies by opening your "inner" ear (clairaudience). You will only be entering a light meditative state, with stilled awareness, to listen to encouragement from the angels.

Exercise 2 EXPLORING ANGEL ENERGIES

- **You will need:** a candle, flowers (optional).

- **Sit in a comfortable meditation posture**—somewhere peaceful and quiet where you will not be disturbed. Set your intent to "listening to the angels."

- **Light a candle** and, if you have an altar, place some flowers as offerings to the angels.

- **Breathe in deeply.** Hold the breath, then let it out slowly. Repeat three times.

- **Loosen your shoulders.** Smile. Close your eyes. You will be surprised at how many angelic voices you will hear whispering sweet encouragement in your ear.

- **Be still, be calm, listen.** You will find that nothing more is needed than an open mind and an open heart. Realize that there is no challenge you face that the angels cannot assist you with.

- **Allow yourself to come back slowly**, in your own time, by taking a few slow, centering breaths.

- **Write down what you experienced** in the space opposite.

My exploring angel energies experience

Date _____   Time _____

I saw _____
_____
_____
_____
_____
_____

I felt _____
_____
_____
_____
_____

I learned _____
_____
_____
_____
_____
_____

My exploring angel energies experience

Date _____ **Time** _____

I saw _____
_____
_____
_____
_____
_____
_____

I felt _____
_____
_____
_____
_____
_____

I learned _____
_____
_____
_____
_____
_____
_____

My exploring angel energies experience

Date _____ **Time** _____

I saw _____
_____
_____
_____
_____
_____
_____

I felt _____
_____
_____
_____
_____
_____

I learned _____
_____
_____
_____
_____
_____

Tuning into the angels of the spheres

In this exercise you begin to raise your consciousness and set the scene to commune regularly with the angels of the spheres. The focus of the exercise is to learn heart-consciousness (clairsentience)—this is the only true way to communicate with the angelic realm.

A simple way is to touch the center of your chest area and let your focus rest there for a few moments. Rose quartz (see page 62) is an excellent crystal to hold during this meditation and will always assist you in connecting to the angels.

Exercise 3 ANGELS OF THE SPHERES AWARENESS

- **You will need:** a candle, pink flowers (optional).

- **Sit on a cushion or chair** in your meditation space.

- **Light a candle** and, if you have an altar, place some pink flowers as offerings to the angels.

- **Give yourself permission to relax.** Free your heart of any worries, doubts, or fears, as you begin to focus gently on your breathing; let it become a little deeper and slower than normal.

- **Release any tension** in your neck, shoulders, hands, feet, and at the base of your spine.

- **Relax deeply and aim for feelings of gentleness and love** as you let your awareness flow to your heart chakra in the center of your body. As it does so, feel your mind becoming tranquil and serene.

- **Issue a silent heartfelt invitation to the angels** to draw near to you, as your serenity deepens.

- **Allow your aura to expand** and fill the space around you. As it does so, feel and see a peaceful, pure pink flame beginning to glow right in the center of your heart chakra. As you watch in fascination, the flame grows a little bigger and brighter. This flame is the innermost chamber of your heart, and this beautiful paradise is where the angels will surround you with their loving embrace.

- **Imagine you can listen to the angels** and speak to them with the voice of your heart.

- **Rest there a while** and realize that you have certainly made contact with your angels. Any time you need to contact them, focus on your breathing, still your mind, and place your awareness deep in the center of your heart chakra, for nothing has the power to stop this blissful communication.

- **Allow yourself to come back slowly**, taking your time and gently grounding yourself (see page 34).

- **Write down what you have experienced** in the space overleaf.

My angels of the spheres awareness experience

Date _____ **Time** _____

I saw _____

_____

_____

_____

_____

_____

I felt _____

_____

_____

_____

_____

_____

I learned _____

_____

_____

_____

_____

_____

My angels of the spheres awareness experience

Date _____ **Time** _____

I saw _____
_____
_____
_____
_____
_____

I felt _____
_____
_____
_____
_____

I learned _____
_____
_____
_____
_____
_____

Meditating on the archangels

The archangels are powerful agents of Divine love. Reconnecting yourself to the natural world where nonhuman forces are more obviously dominant compared to an urban environment, can be a very effective way to attune yourself to cosmic energy. The following exercise will help you reconnect with nature.

Exercise 4 ARCHANGELS MEDITATION

- **You will need:** a rug (optional).

- **Choose a cloudless evening in midsummer** when there is a full moon.

- **Visit a beautiful outdoor space**—it could be a local park or you may wish to make a special journey to the countryside.

- **Spend the evening seated on a rug** or the bare grass if you prefer. Close your eyes and bring yourself into a calm, meditative state as described in Exercise 1.

- **Now open your eyes and gaze at the setting sun in all its glory.** Feel its lingering rays warm your cheeks. Acknowledge its magnificence and power as it sets below the horizon.

- **Observe as the evening stars begin to emerge one by one.** Bow your head to each as they appear in turn.

- **Wait for the rising of the full moon.** Close your eyes and take several deep breaths as it rises over the horizon.

- **Open your eyes and give thanks to the Divine**—all that contains this cosmic energy.

- **Write about your experience** when you get home using the form opposite.

My archangels meditation experience

Date _____ Time _____

I saw _____

_____

_____

_____

_____

_____

I felt _____

_____

_____

_____

_____

I learned _____

_____

_____

_____

_____

_____

My archangels meditation experience

Date _____ **Time** _____

I saw _____
_____
_____
_____
_____
_____
_____

I felt _____
_____
_____
_____
_____
_____

I learned _____
_____
_____
_____
_____
_____
_____

CONNECTING
WITH ANGELS

Angels and chakras

One of the most important ways to access angel energy is through understanding and working with your chakras, the subtle energy centers found at various points along your body. The chakras link us to the world of spirit—and the more we are in tune with them the easier it will be to communicate with the angelic world.

There are seven master chakras in the human body, with the first five (running from the root to the throat chakras) being embedded in the spinal column. Each of the chakras vibrates at a different frequency and is ruled by an archangel with a corresponding color ray, element, and qualities.

Focusing on each of the chakras while you meditate can be a very effective way to bring your angel closer. You can choose to meditate sitting on a chair or lying down. Some people also find choosing simple yoga poses that complement the chakra can provide a deeper focus and more profound experience.

Crown chakra

Third-eye chakra

Throat chakra

Heart chakra

Solar-plexus chakra

Sacral chakra

Root chakra

The seven chakras and their associations

Chakra (Sanskrit name)	Color ray	Element	Archangel	Qualities
Root chakra (muladhara)	Ruby-red	Earth	Uriel	Groundedness and stability
Sacral chakra (svadhisthana)	Orange	Water	Gabriel	Creativity and originality
Solar-plexus chakra (manipuraka)	Yellow	Fire	Jophiel	Confidence and manifestation
Heart chakra (anahata)	Green	Air	Raphael	Balance and harmony
Throat chakra (visuddha)	Blue	Ether	Michael	Communication and self-expression
Third-eye chakra (ajna)	Indigo	Avyakta*	Raziel	Intuition and clairvoyance
Crown chakra (sahasrara)	Violet	Cosmic energy	Zadkiel	Cosmic consciousness

* Avyakta = "primordial cloud of undifferentiated light"

> **Work with your angels now** To develop awareness of each of the chakras in turn and become sensitive to the energy of each, turn to Exercise 5: Chakra Awareness Visualization on pages 66–67.

Yoga poses and the chakras

In the Hindu and Buddhist traditions, yoga poses were developed to enhance the energy of each chakra and to bring about internal balance. The simple poses below are suitable for beginners but can also take your awareness of chakra energy to a much deeper level.

Base chakra

Kneel on a yoga mat with your legs hip-width apart, your buttocks resting on your heels, and your hands resting on your thighs. Lengthen the back of your neck by tucking in your chin. Close your eyes and breathe deeply. Stay quietly in this pose for as long as it feels comfortable. Imagine a red light shining down from your base chakra into the center of the Earth.

Sacral chakra

While you practice this pose, imagine an orange light radiating from your sacral chakra. Lie on your back on your mat, with your knees bent and your feet flat on the mat. Place your arms by your sides, palms down. Inhale, allowing the small of your back to touch the mat. Exhale, pressing the small of your back into the mat. This creates a gentle rocking movement. Move your arms slightly away from your body and, keeping the soles of your feet together, exhale while lowering your right knee to the floor. Inhale and draw your knee back up. Repeat with your left knee. Repeat three times on each side. Now gently lower both knees to the floor, keeping the soles of your feet together and breathing deeply into your pelvic area.

Solar plexus chakra

Stand with your feet slightly wider than hip-width apart. Slightly bend your knees, bend forward, and rest your hands on your knees. Inhale and exhale thoroughly. Pull in your abdomen toward your spine. Hold for as long as possible while keeping your lungs empty. Come out of the pose when you are ready and stand upright. Inhale and exhale slowly, then repeat the pose three more times.

Heart chakra

As you do this pose, imagine a green light radiating from your chest. Stand with your feet hip-width apart and your neck elongated. Inhale and stretch out your arms at shoulder height, your palms facing forward. Exhale. As you inhale, stretch your arms backward without bending your elbows. Lift your chin and raise your chest. Exhale, bringing your arms forward until your palms meet. Curve your upper back forward. Repeat this pose several times, then finish with an exhalation as you slowly lower your arms to your sides.

Throat chakra

Imagine blue light emanating from the front of the chakra when you perform this pose. Sit cross-legged on your yoga mat. Inhale, then lower your chin until it presses against your chest. Hold your breath for a few moments, then exhale. When you are ready, inhale while raising your head again.

Third-eye chakra

Rub your hands together and cup them over your closed eyes for a few seconds. Gradually open your fingers, then open your eyes and lower your hands. Moving only your eyes, imagine you are looking at a clock face, starting with 12 and 6 o'clock, then 3 and 9 o'clock, followed by every other opposing pair of numbers. Look up and down at each set of numbers five times. Squeeze your eyes shut, then relax them, several times, before moving on to the next set of numbers. Finish by looking into the far distance, then the middle distance five times, before cupping your hands in front of your eyes again.

Crown chakra

Kneel on a mat and bend forward until your head rests on the mat (this is called the Child pose). Place your palms flat on the mat on either side of your knees. Inhale, raising your buttocks so the crown of your head rests on the mat, and exhale. Inhale, clasping your hands behind you and raising them as high as possible. Exhale, and hold the pose for as long as is comfortable. Imagine a violet light radiating from your crown chakra. Exhale and gently return to the Child pose. Rest for a few minutes, breathing quietly, before sitting up.

Work with your angels now
Once you have completed your chakra workout, turn to Exercise 6: Activating your Angelic Chakra on pages 70–71 to learn how to activate your angelic chakra.

I'm not quite there yet If you don't yet feel in tune with your chakras repeat Exercise 5: Chakra Awareness Visualization on page 66 to raise your awareness.

Crystals and the angels

My two great passions are angels and crystals. I have taught professional crystal-therapy courses internationally since 1986 and have trained thousands of people to use crystals to enhance all areas of their lives. Crystals and angels work together in perfect harmony. The crystals give you a tangible item to hold that can enable you to feel more empowered to connect with the angelic realm, or directly with specific angels.

If you wish to connect with the angelic realm through the assistance of crystals, you can use selenite (see page 61) because of its gentleness; it opens up the higher chakras, enabling the angelic realm's unconditional love and knowledge to simply flow through you; or you can think of it as dripping through—like coffee through a filter, slowly filling up the pot and, before you know it, the pot is full. What a great tool to have in a room where you meditate or see clients, or in any room in which you spend a lot of time.

Crystals and gemstones have been used for thousands of years for decoration, physical adornment, healing, protection, magic, scrying (foretelling the future), and religious ceremonies. They are the most organized and stable examples of physical matter in the natural world, and represent the lowest possible state of entropy (disorder). All crystalline structures are made up of mathematically precise, three-dimensional arrangements of atoms, and this crystal lattice confers a high level of stability. It also gives crystals their unique colors, hardness, and physical, geometrical, and subtle-energetic properties. Gemstones and crystals have an amazing capacity to absorb, store, reflect, and radiate light in the form of intelligent fields of stable energy that can increase the flow of vital life-force within the human body. By applying this stable energy or crystal resonance in a coherent, focused way to dysfunctional energy systems, you can use crystals to restore stability and balance.

Crystals have a unique aura of mystery and magic. They never lose their color, brilliance, beauty, or value, and in many ancient civilizations this aligned them with the spirit world and with Heaven. Crystals are mentioned many times in the Bible, and in metaphysical circles it is believed that certain crystals are naturally attuned to the angelic realm because of their color, appearance, or name (such as angelite or celestite). They also have a very high resonance, which naturally attunes the wearer to the highest spiritual realms.

Over the next few pages we will explore the most beautiful angelic crystals you can imagine, and in the exercises you will use them to cleanse and activate your angelic chakra (see pages 70–71).

Azeztulite

Azeztulite is either clear or opaque, but it is extremely rare in either state. It is a very high-energy form of quartz that has been repatterned and activated by the Angels of the Azez, who work extensively with azeztulite. The Angels of the Azez are aligned with the "Great Central Sun" and are present at many of the etheric realm's major power centers, including the Andes and the Himalayas. They work with an energy known as "Nameless Light." Azeztulite can trigger huge shifts in consciousness that are particularly helpful when giving healing, and it also helps to dissolve old emotional patterns. In addition, it can stimulate conscious inter-dimensional travel. As a result, it should be used with care. When you work or meditate with azeztulite, or wear it, you become part of the network of "Nameless Light" that helps to raise the consciousness of all humanity.

Danburite

Danburite is a beautiful, transparent crystal that may be clear in color, a soft pink, or a delicate green. It is easily obtained and is therefore a wonderful addition to any collection of crystals, because it has such a wide range of healing energies, making it a cure-all. It operates at an extremely high vibration that attracts Divine light, swiftly opens the heart and crown chakras, stimulates lucid dreaming (a state in which someone is consciously aware of being in a dream), and enables us to connect easily with the angelic realm. Danburite has a very beneficial impact on the aura, helping to improve any difficult conditions that have led to unhappiness and "dis-ease," and is particularly helpful when clearing the body of allergies and toxins. In addition to healing, danburite has many other uses, including spiritual awakening, inspiration, soul purification, and guidance. Its energies are perfectly attuned to the Archangel Gabriel.

Celestite

This beautiful crystal, which is also known as celestina or celestita, gets its name from its celestial blue coloring. It has very strong links with the Celestial Guardians, which are the massive light-beings that guide the cosmos, and is therefore an ideal crystal for attuning with the angelic realm. People who work with celestite are able to create and maintain a continual connection with the angels. Celestite has many uses, but is particularly effective at calming the emotions and bringing inner peace. It is of great benefit to people who act like sponges, soaking up the emotional turmoil and problems of others. When working on a physical level, it soothes all nervous and stress-induced ailments; on a psychological level, celestite fosters joy, harmony, and communication skills. It also releases creative blockages, helping you to connect more easily with the angels and to receive insights from them.

Angelite

Angelite (also known as blue anhydrite) was created over millions of years from compressed celestite. It is opaque, with white veining, and is often carved into miniature angels that can be carried in a pocket or placed on an altar. In addition, it can physically represent the energies of your own guardian angel. Angelite is a marvelous crystal for attuning to and also communicating with the angelic realm, enhancing telepathy and creating a sense of peace, and this is why it is highly prized by spiritual healers and mediums. It emits a calming, loving vibration that encourages tranquility, kindness, compassion as well as benevolence. On a mental level it has a grounding effect, enabling you to focus on the present moment. In healing, when angelite is held against the feet and hands, it clears the meridians (energy channels) and helps to remove any energy blockages.

Selenite

This powerful crystal is available as a clear gemstone and in a shape that looks like a rosette. In its translucent form it carries the imprint of everything that has happened in our world. Above all, selenite is a crystal that aids communication, especially with the past and the present. It helps you to establish telepathic links and is useful when you want to create a strong connection with your spirit guides and with your higher self. It also enables you to recall your past lives, is beneficial in meditation, and helps when remembering your dreams. In addition, it opens the portals to other dimensions for initiation and for "light-body" activation. A selenite wand contains ancient healing secrets, helping healers to scan someone's aura, dissolve energy blockages, and discover the spiritual reason for those blocks. Selenite also quickly opens the third-eye, crown, and soul-star chakras. It has strong connections with the Archangel Auriel and the angels of the moon.

Apophyllite

This crystal encourages a deep inner peace that spreads through your entire being and aura, and is therefore very helpful when you are having difficulty in sleeping or when you simply want to dream more sweetly. It also helps to lift your consciousness into higher planes of awareness. All forms of apophyllite carry the vibrations of the higher realms and are excellent when you want to attune to the angels. When applied to the third-eye chakra or the angelic chakra during meditation, an apophyllite pyramid will trigger waves of comforting angelic energy. Such pyramids are powerful energizers that enhance spiritual awareness during meditation. Green apophyllite is particularly useful for connecting with nature spirits on a telepathic level.

Rose quartz

This beautiful pink crystal is naturally attuned to the heart chakra, so it helps you to establish stronger connections with the people in your life, as well as to appreciate the loving relationships you already enjoy. Rose quartz is beneficial for relationships of every kind and is especially helpful when you are weathering the upheavals involved in life-changing situations, such as divorce and bereavement. Soothing and comforting, rose quartz helps to prevent the bottling up of disruptive emotions such as jealousy; it releases aggressive behavior patterns and enables you to dissolve feelings of low self-esteem or selfishness. During meditation, rose quartz may be placed on the heart chakra or on any other area of the body that is holding tension or pain. Rose quartz resonates with the Archangel Chamuel and with the angels of love and devotion.

Angel-aura quartz™

A manufactured crystal, angel-aura quartz™ is created by bonding natural quartz crystals with platinum, to produce a shimmering range of iridescent pale rainbow colors that give you psychic protection. It is therefore an excellent crystal to wear when you want to protect your aura. This crystal enables you to quickly make contact with the angelic realm, and to connect with the "inner temple" of your higher self in order to gain knowledge of your guardian angel. It is associated with a group of celestial crystal beings that give guidance and help to people who use crystals during meditation and therapy sessions. On a psychological level, angel-aura quartz™ helps you to appreciate the beauty around you and increases your awareness of nature spirits and fairies, as well as creating a sense of lightness and spontaneity.

Seriphos green quartz

Ranging in color from pale jade to an intense green, this crystal quickly attunes you to the healing qualities of the celestial realms. It is particularly helpful for healing a broken heart because it fosters emotional stability, and is used to open, cleanse, and activate the heart center. Seriphos green quartz also brings abundance, balance, and harmony. It is a very useful crystal for anyone who is uncomfortable in their physical body.

Seraphinite

This dark-green crystal, which is also known as clinochlore, aligns the physical, etheric, and astral bodies. It is beneficial when establishing angelic connections, particularly with the Archangel Seraphiel. Seraphinite clears away thought forms that have become stuck in the mental body and has a grounding effect. It also harmonizes the desires of your heart with those of your soul.

Moldavite

Moldavite is a dark-green crystal that works on all the chakras, but it works especially well with the heart chakra. It has a powerful transformational quality, bringing spiritual breakthrough and accelerating your personal evolution. Because Moldavite has no structure it can take you beyond your limiting self-belief system into uncharted realms of infinite possibilities.

 Work with your angels now For exercises using these crystals, turn to Exercise 7: Angelic Crystal Meditation on pages 74–75 and Exercise 8: Angelic Alignment using a Crystal on pages 78–79.

I'm not quite there yet If you're not sure about which crystal is working best for you, try Exercise 2: Exploring Angel Energies on page 38 and then select a crystal at random. This may be the crystal that will best meet your needs.

EXERCISES TO CONNECT WITH ANGELS

The following exercises are designed to enhance your connection with angels, either through greater awareness of the chakras and the spiritual principles they embody, or through crystals, essential tools for angel work.

Chakra awareness

The chakras are your own personal link to the world of spirit. The more you understand and work with each of the chakras the more sensitive you will become to angels and angel energy.

This exercise is designed to develop your awareness of the quality of each of the chakras in turn. Turn to page 50 for a visual reference for the location of each chakra if you are uncertain.

Exercise 5 CHAKRA AWARENESS VISUALIZATION

- **Lie on the floor with your shoulders relaxed,** your arms away from your body, and your legs slightly apart. Take a few breaths deep into your belly. With each out breath feel yourself relax further. Close your eyes.

- **Place your hand gently over the base chakra.** Breathe deeply and focus on the color red. Feel yourself connecting to the earth and feeling grounded and stable.

- **Move your hand to the sacral chakra,** over your belly. Focus on the color orange and feel your energy grow. Breathe deeply as you reflect on your powers of originality and creativity.

- **Move your hand up to your solar plexus chakra.** Focus on the color yellow and feel confident and aware.

- **Now move your hand to your heart chakra** and focus on the color green. Feel yourself in balance and harmony, full of love and compassion.

- **Now to your throat chakra.** In your mind's eye see the color blue and focus on communication and your ability to express your innermost thoughts and identity.

- **Move your hand to your brow chakra.** Concentrate on the color indigo and let your mind run freely, exploring where it will.

- **Finally place your hand lightly on the crown chakra.** Focus on the color violet but otherwise let your mind be completely blank. Stay in this position for 5 minutes.

- **Gently open your eyes** and bring yourself back to the here and now. Record your experiences on the pages overleaf.

My chakra awareness visualization experience

Date _____ **Time** _____

I saw _____
_____
_____
_____
_____
_____

I felt _____
_____
_____
_____
_____
_____

I learned _____
_____
_____
_____
_____
_____
_____

My chakra awareness visualization experience

Date _____ Time _____

I saw _____
_____
_____
_____
_____
_____
_____

I felt _____
_____
_____
_____
_____
_____

I learned _____
_____
_____
_____
_____
_____

Activating your angelic chakra

The following exercise will open, purify, and activate your angelic chakra. Most people do not realize they have an angelic chakra. This sacred center is located just above your third-eye chakra, at the very top of your forehead.

 Exercise 6 ACTIVATING YOUR ANGELIC CHAKRA CD REFERENCE TRACK 2

- **You will need:** a yoga mat to lie on, a small angelic crystal, such as an apophyllite pyramid (if you do not have one, use a small clear quartz crystal instead); make sure your crystal has been cleansed (see page 74)

- **Lie down and make yourself comfortable,** allowing your eyes to close and breathing slowly and deeply. Let your body relax completely. Release any tension in your neck, shoulders, hands, feet, and at the base of your spine.

- **Listen to the sound of my voice** and begin to go into deeper states of relaxation.

- **Feel yourself sinking deeper and deeper** into a state of relaxation and peace. Let your aura expand to fill the space around you.

- **To assist you in this process, call on** your angels, your guardian angel, or the Archangel Raphael.

- **Place your crystal on your angelic chakra** once you sense the presence of your angels surrounding you with their energy.

- **Feel the angelic chakra opening,** purifying and activating itself.

- **Consider how you feel physically:** is there any part of your body that draws your attention?

- **Now move to your emotions:** what mood are you feeling?

- **And now focus on your thoughts:** what is the quality of your thoughts like?

- **Finish by grounding yourself** (see page 34) when you are ready to conclude the session.

- **Write down what you experienced** in the space overleaf.

My angelic-chakra activation experience

Date _____ **Time** _____

I saw _____
_____
_____
_____
_____
_____

I felt _____
_____
_____
_____
_____
_____

I learned _____
_____
_____
_____
_____
_____
_____

My angelic-chakra activation experience

Date _____ Time _____

I saw _____
_____
_____
_____
_____
_____

I felt _____
_____
_____
_____
_____

I learned _____
_____
_____
_____
_____
_____

Crystal meditation

This meditation enables you to meet your crystal-guide. The first few times you try this, you may not be able to meet the crystal-spirit in any form that is definite. However, after several explorations using the same crystal—setting out with the same intention of meeting the crystal energy in a form that you can communicate with—you should get results that you can understand. Be clear in your intent and focus your mind on an angelic encounter.

It is important to purify your crystal before and after use to remove any residual disharmonies and fill it with life-affirming vibrations. You can do this by passing the crystal through smoke (keep a window open to let the stagnant energy out); using sound in the form of a crystal singing bowl, a bell, ting sha (small Tibetan cymbals), or a tuning fork; or using specialty aromatherapy cleansers; even tap water will do in an emergency.

Exercise 7 ANGELIC CRYSTAL MEDITATION

- **You will need:** an angelic crystal (if you have none of those listed on pages 59–64, use a clear quartz crystal); make sure your crystal has been cleansed.

- **Sit on a cushion or chair** in your meditation space.

- **Hold the crystal you are working with** in your nondominant, receiving hand.

- **Give yourself permission to relax** and let go of all your worries, fears, and concerns, letting your heart feel free of all self-doubt.

- **Gently focus on your breathing,** letting it become a little deeper and slower than normal.

- **Allow your eyes to close** and release any tension in your neck, shoulders, hands, feet, and at the base of your spine.

- **Imagine the mouth of a cave in front of you.** Take some time to build the image clearly.

- **Picture yourself going into the cave.** Move slowly and allow your impressions of the cave to form.

- **Move further into the cave,** and see in front of you a path leading downward.

- **Keep following the path,** and you will eventually arrive at a door.

- **Imagine an image of your crystal** or the name of the crystal on the door.

- **Focus your intention to meet your crystal-guide,** then see the door opening.

- **Step through the doorway** and gather your impressions. Take time to explore and meet your guide.

- **Say "thank you" when it's time to return,** and retrace your steps out of the cave.

- **Write down what you experienced** in the space overleaf.

My angelic crystal meditation experience

Date _____ **Time** _____

I felt _____
_____
_____
_____
_____
_____

I saw _____
_____
_____
_____
_____
_____

I learned _____
_____
_____
_____
_____
_____

My angelic crystal meditation experience

Date _____ **Time** _____

I felt _____
_____
_____
_____
_____
_____

I saw _____
_____
_____
_____
_____

I learned _____
_____
_____
_____
_____
_____

Angelic alignment

The crystal that you use for this angelic alignment exercise will absorb and store the angelic energy from this meditation. Keep it on your altar, if you have one, and hold it whenever you need an angelic energy boost.

 Exercise 8 ANGELIC ALIGNMENT USING A CRYSTAL CD REFERENCE TRACK 3

- **You will need:** an angelic crystal such as danburite or selenite (if you have neither of these, use a clear quartz crystal instead); make sure your crystal has been cleansed (see page 74).

- **Sit in a comfortable meditation posture** and relax your body by focusing on your breathing.

- **Listen to the sound of my voice** and allow yourself to relax completely.

- **Take a few moments to look closely at your crystal,** once you have relaxed. Hold it in both hands and imagine breathing in and out of the crystal for a minute or two.

- **Begin to feel the crystal energy building up** in your heart center.

- **Breathe this energy outward and upward,** sending it up to Heaven, and with it send gratitude for all the good things in your life.

- **Imagine an overcast day,** then see the clouds part, as a ray of brilliant white light comes through and settles directly on your head.

- **Absorb the light into your being** through the top of your head. This is your link with the angelic realm.

- **Let celestial light pour through your body;** feel it nurturing every cell.

- **Bring in all the angelic blessings** in the form of light that are meant for you, as you now focus on your heart chakra.

- **It is now time to make full contact with your angelic guidance.** From the deepest center of your heart, where your Divine spark dwells, send out your longing for an angel to be your guide.

- **Feel your angel drawing closer,** and imagine it standing beside you and enfolding you with its beautiful wings. Feel the unconditional love that your angel is directing toward you—this energy forms a sphere of brilliant golden light around you. It will protect you and shield you from all negativity and harm. Stay in this energy as long as you wish.

- **Allow the image to fade from view** when you are ready, but be aware that your angel is beside you.

- **Conclude the session** by bringing yourself back to everyday waking reality.

- **Write down what you experienced** on the space overleaf.

My angelic-alignment using a crystal experience

Date _____ **Time** _____

I saw _____
_____
_____
_____
_____
_____

I felt _____
_____
_____
_____
_____
_____

I learned _____
_____
_____
_____
_____
_____
_____

WELCOMING
ANGELS

Angel visions

Stories sprinkled throughout this book show that angels can take many forms and come in many guises. We have all heard stories of angels appearing in human form, but we don't always recognize them as angels at the time of their appearance. Sometimes it is only when we look back that we realize we have had an angel experience. As the Bible tells us in Hebrews 13:2: "Do not neglect to show hospitality to strangers, for by that some have entertained angels without knowing it."

Most people are familiar with angels through religious art, where they are depicted as perfect beings, with long flowing robes, long hair, haloes, and wings, but angels are pure spirit and therefore have no gross physical form. The angels I see are certainly beautiful, and they mostly appear to be very tall, elegant, and majestic. They radiate the love and glory of the Holy Spirit and, like all angels, are androgynous in appearance, not showing any specific gender.

My guardian angel appears as tall, elegant, and impressive, with a dignified, loving presence, a graceful smile on its lips, and a twinkle in the eyes. It appears to wear crystalline robes of light, and the majestic wings are magnificent. A student of mine sees angels as pure, dazzling, pearly-white light, which emanates from the arch of their white silver-tipped wings to reveal the outline of an exquisitely beautiful being inside.

When teaching groups of students, or during therapy sessions, we often see radiating, pulsing spheres of iridescent light, in a multitude of sizes and rainbow colors. In the center of each are geometric shapes—these are intricate, filigree fibers of flowing energy, which then arrange themselves into multi-petaled flowers or kaleidoscopic wheels. These angelic spheres dance joyously around the students and seem to delight in the group energy. Words seem totally inadequate to capture the true description of an angel.

The group of books known as *The Sepher Zohar* (or simply *The Zohar*) (see page 86), which contains a mystical discussion on the nature of God, states

that "whenever the celestial spirits descend to Earth, they clothe themselves in corporeal elements and appear to men in human shape."

This chapter explores the ways in which we can encourage angels into our world and how to recognize when they have visited us.

 Work with your angels now To explore your own angel vision, turn to Exercise 9: Your Angel Vision on page 98.

I'm not quite there yet Revisit Exercises 1–6 (pages 34–48 and 66–71) to help you connect to the angel realm.

Creating an angel altar

Angels are attracted like magnets to places by the energies of love, joy, and peace. It is important to create a sacred space within your home where you plan to meditate on and connect with your angels and that this space be as beautiful and harmonious as possible.

Your altar is an important link, establishing a powerful connection with the celestial realms. It will become a tangible focus—a portal to serenity, somewhere you can still your mind and open your heart to the angels. It will quickly become your own sacred space; a sanctuary for your soul that is charged with harmonious energy; somewhere you can come each day to seek renewal. Creating this angel altar grounds your spiritual transformation, providing you with an opportunity to explore your creativity and express yourself emotionally and artistically.

To create your own altar, cover a small, low table with a cloth or scarf. Place on it the items that inspire you, such as crystals, angelic art, photographs of loved ones or spiritual teachers, bells, incense, flowers, candles, religious icons, angel cards or feathers. Include a representation of anything you wish to bring into your life, such as love, spiritual wisdom, or abundance. Let your sacred space evolve over time, as you develop your angelic awareness by inviting the sacred into your life.

Remember that individual angels are associated with particular colors, crystals, zodiac signs, and more (see *The Angel Bible* for a complete guide to angel correspondences) so if you would like to attract a particular angel, Gabriel for example, you might choose a shining white silk cloth to drape over your table and decorate it with a danburite crystal.

> **Work with your angels now** For a guided meditation to bless your sacred space, turn to Exercise 10: Angel Altar Blessing on page 100.

The Kabala

This form of Jewish mysticism is a rich source of angelic lore. Although the Kabala can at first seem complicated it is another important tool in helping you better understand the angelic realm and connect with it. There are two key manuscripts: *The Zohar* or "Book of Splendor" and *The Sepher Yetzirah* or "Book of Formation."

Jewish folklore claims that God taught the Kabala to the angels before he created the physical world. The teachings were given to Adam and Eve by Archangel Raziel to enable them to return once again to Paradise. The Kabalist structure of existence shows the descending logical stages through which God manifested the original Divine scheme. Each of the ten stages, or *sephiroth* (singular *sephirah*), is ruled over by an archangel. The diagram opposite shows what is known as "the tree of life"—Kabala mystics consider this as a manifestation of the essential

structure of existence. It can be seen as a path to the Divine that you reach by working your way through each *sephirah*. By meditating on the tree of life and the qualities associated with each *sephirah* you will be drawing closer to the angels' own world and the energies within.

 **Work with your angels now** For a tree of life-inspired visualization, turn to Exercise 11: Tree of Life Meditation on pages 102–103.

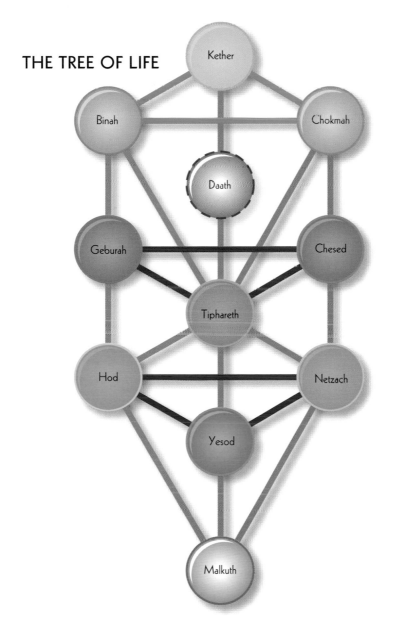

THE TREE OF LIFE

Kether

Binah

Chokmah

Daath

Geburah

Chesed

Tiphareth

Hod

Netzach

Yesod

Malkuth

Creating an angel prayer

As St. Thomas Aquinas (the angelic doctor, 1225–1274) wrote: "Angels transcend every religion, every philosophy, every creed. In fact angels have no religion as we know it. Their existence precedes every religious system that has existed on Earth."

It is vital to remember that angels were created as an extension of the Divine's consciousness, so it is all right to pray to the angels, for they link directly to the Divine. Prayer is a powerful thing —not simply an invocation, but an opportunity to enter whole-heartedly into a powerful communication with the creative force of the universe. Through prayer you become a living channel for the unity of love.

Prayer is an act of intent to establish your connection to the Divine source of love, and a chance to surrender your worries and cares. The Divine does not require your worship, only your love.

Prayers to the angels are about manifestation and guidance and, more importantly, inspiration. Your prayers should include your gratitude for all the good things in your life. They can be very personal, and need not be spoken out loud; in fact, the speech of angels is a form of direct communication from one angel to another—intellectual communication— so you can easily communicate mentally with your angel. Angels are all-compassionate, loving, and giving, great sources of harmony and light.

Your prayers may either be written down or made up as you go along. Write some down in your angelic journal. You can pray every day, or with groups of like-minded people. Some prayers are designed to be said for a specific length of time. A novena (from the Latin for "nine") is a devotion consisting of prayers said on nine successive days, asking to obtain special graces (the supernatural help of God).

Sound and angels

The angels can also be attracted to you by the power of sound. On a cosmic scale, sound is a universal unseen power, able to bring about profound changes on many levels. The 22 letters of the Hebrew alphabet consist entirely of consonants, and they are considered sacred. These consonants have a vibration or energy signature, which means that they are alive with creative cosmic power. This cosmic power is latent and can only be activated by the human voice when it provides the vowel sounds. Kabalists (see page 86) emphasize that prayer is not effective unless it is spoken aloud. Speaking aloud, they believe, releases the cosmic force of the Divine. This then flows down through the sephiroth of the tree of life, and then through the individual speaking aloud. This then allows the "Will of God" to be made manifest on Earth.

Sound is generated as a vibratory motion of particles and objects. The vibrations that produce sound exhibit an energy— a sonic vibratory pattern—that is found throughout nature. Many cultures and religions revere sound so deeply that they believe it called the universe into being. The vibrational patterns of sound possess the key to understanding the patterns of being and the organization of matter in the physical universe.

Archangel Shamael is the angel of sacred sound. He is depicted as an aspect of Archangel Metatron, who rules over the *sephirah* of Kether, or crown, in the Kabalistic mystical tradition. He represents the first impetus of creation.

Invoke Archangel Shamael to practice sacred sound, by using your voice for chanting, mantras, or devotional singing, or for playing a Himalayan or quartz-crystal singing bowl.

Physical associations Shamael relaxes the body and induces alpha brain waves; lowers blood pressure and heart rate.

Emotional and mental associations Shamael calms the mind, and heals through sympathetic vibration.

Spiritual associations Shamael uplifts and renews the spirit; and aids meditation.

 **Work with your angels now** For an exercise using the power of sound, turn to Exercise 12: Sound Meditation on page 106.

Angelic mantras

Mantras are the next stage in focusing your use of sound to attract angels. Mantras have been used for eons as tools for spiritual development. In Indian religions, a mantra is a sound, syllable, word, or group of words capable of creating transformation. Its type and use vary greatly—mantras are used in religious ceremonies to accumulate wealth, avoid danger, or eliminate enemies. The practice of chanting mantras is now widespread in various spiritual movements. The most basic mantra is *Aum*, which focuses on the "one reality." A mantra is usually repeated an auspicious number of times —108 is the norm—and for this reason Hindu mala beads have been developed, so that you can count the number of repetitions. My own mala is made of pure, clear quartz crystal. You can also use one of the popular prayer bead bracelets available on the Internet.

Most religious traditions have what is called a "centering prayer." You could create something similar using words that are sacred to you, or an affirmation (a positive statement that you repeat to yourself to harness the power of positive thinking). Sacred words can be very simple, but they must be heartfelt, such as "love," "peace," or "serenity." Simply repeat them as many times as you wish and, at the end, spend several minutes focusing on any differences in your awareness that you perceive. A simple angelic healing "mantra" might be: "Heal, soothe, calm."

A healing angel affirmation might be: "I align myself with the energies of Archangel Raphael and am healed, with Divine love and Grace, perfectly aligned and balanced on all levels of being." Or, for soul development: "I align myself with the energy of Archangel Raziel and am sublimely guided to explore, understand secrets, and experience the magic of creation."

I always suggest that you write your affirmation on a piece of paper and place it under a clear quartz-crystal standing point (the flat end on which the crystal will stand up). This amplifies the affirmation and assists your spiritual development.

Temples of light

Another way to draw closer to angels is to learn more about their "temples of light" or ashrams. This is their spiritual home and is anchored in the etheric, over the Earth's various "power" vortexes. These ashrams were established by the "spiritual hierarchy" under the guidance of the archangels—in times long forgotten, when angels walked the Earth side-by-side with humans. Each temple has a different purpose that can help you on your spiritual path.

The focus of each ashram relates to a "cosmic virtue" that each archangel enshrines (see pages 28–31 for the list of virtues bestowed by the various archangels). When spiritual seekers visit the ashram during meditation, they are nourished and inspired.

The locations and associated colors of some of the most well known are given on page 96, for you to use in your healing meditation.

 **Work with your angels now** Turn to Exercise 13: Angel Temple Meditation on pages 108–109 for a temple of light guided meditation.

The archangels and their temples

Archangel	Temple location	Color
Archangel Azrael	Inner sanctum, Stonehenge, Wiltshire, UK	Iridescent black
Archangel Cassiel	Saturn, guardian of the threshold	Dark blue
Archangel Chamuel	St. Louis, Missouri, USA	Pink
Archangel Gabriel	Mount Shasta, California, USA	Orange
Archangel Haniel	Himalayas, Tibet	Turquoise
Archangel Jophiel	Lanchow, China	Yellow
Archangel Melchizedek	Jerusalem, Israel	White-gold
Archangel Metatron	Luxor, Egypt	Iridescent white
Archangel Michael	Paradise Valley, Banff, Canada	Cobalt blue
Archangel Raphael	Fatima, Portugal	Emerald green
Archangel Raziel	Pacific Ocean (where Lemuria flourished)	Indigo
Archangel Sandalphon	El Chorro, southern Spain	Rainbow
Archangel Shamael	Luxor, Egypt	Iridescent white
Archangel Tzaphkiel	Atlantic Ocean (where Atlantis flourished)	Magenta
Archangel Uriel	Tatra Mountains, Poland	Flame red
Archangel Zadkiel	Cuba	Violet

EXERCISES TO WELCOME ANGELS

The following exercises will help you draw closer to angels,
encouraging you to understand their own world better and
to begin accessing their energy.

Angel visions

As you begin to connect with the angels you may find your sense of their presence grows stronger. This exercise is designed to help you express the essence of your own angel. You will need drawing paper, and a set of watercolor paints and brushes. These are quite cheap to buy at a local stationer or specialty craft store. You don't need to be worried if you have never painted before. You don't need any particular skill; the exercise is simply designed to allow you to freely express in color and shape your angel vision.

Exercise 9 YOUR ANGEL VISION

- **You will need:** art paper, watercolor paints, paint brush.

- **Close your eyes** and take a few deep breaths.

- **Bring to your mind's eye** the words "angel," "love," "wisdom," and "compassion." Continue to focus on those words for several minutes.

- **Now open your eyes,** pick up your brush and start mixing the colors that first appeal to you.

- **Sweep the brush across the paper** in whatever form feels right to you. You don't need to draw an actual figure—just evoke the mood from your visualization.

- **Stop, put down your brush** and close your eyes again.

- **Open your eyes** and record your response to your watercolor in the form opposite.

My angel vision experience

Date _____ **Time** _____

I saw _____
_____
_____
_____
_____
_____

I felt _____
_____
_____
_____
_____
_____

I learned _____
_____
_____
_____
_____
_____

Altar blessing

It is important to establish a positive energy around your angel altar. You can do that in a number of ways—through music, through the use of traditional chimes or singing bowls, or you may wish to read aloud your favorite poems of love and compassion. The following exercise shows you how to write your own sacred space blessing for your altar.

 ## Exercise 10 ANGEL ALTAR BLESSING
CD REFERENCE TRACK 4

- **Meditate quietly for a few minutes** on all that you want your sacred space to embody—peace, love, and harmony, or perhaps it is spiritual growth and creativity.

- **Play CD track 4** and let the sounds wash over and inspire you.

- **Let your mind drift** and see what particular words or images emerge. Does a particular angel appear in your mind's eye?

- **Write down a draft blessing.** Perhaps this will just be a series of words: "May this space be one of joy, light, love," for example. Or perhaps you will feel moved to write an invocation to a specific angel.

- **Close your eyes and play CD track 4 once more.** Let your mind go blank; don't think about what you have written; just listen to the music.

- **Open your eyes and write a second draft.**

- **Compare the two blessings.** Whichever you think is the strongest write out fully on the page opposite.

My angel altar blessing experience

Date _____ Time _____

I saw _____
_____
_____
_____
_____
_____
_____

I felt _____
_____
_____
_____
_____
_____

I learned _____
_____
_____
_____
_____
_____
_____

Tree of life meditation

This meditation will take you on a journey ascending the tree of life. There are many different possible paths to take and it is well worthwhile exploring different paths on the tree of life in a number of different meditations to see what revelations the different paths can bring.

Exercise 11 TREE OF LIFE MEDITATION

- **Take a few minutes to relax** and breathe deeply as described in Exercise 1, pages 34–35, letting all the tension fall away from your body. Close your eyes.

- **The first *sephirah* is "Malkuth"** or Kingdom and is ruled by the Archangel Sandalphon or Archangel Uriel. Focus on the color red, and feel the energy of power, authority, and guidance that is embodied in Uriel. Now feel the energy of Sandalphon, which spans the entire "tree of life" from top to bottom. Ask to share a little of that connecting energy.

- **Moving up the tree of life you now reach Yesod** or Foundation, ruled by the Archangel Gabriel. Meditate on Gabriel's energy, which is guiding, purifying, and spiritually inspiring. Feel your mind expand as you take in this powerful vibration.

- **You now move to the left, to Hod** or Glory. This is ruled by Archngel Michael or Archangel Jophiel. Feel the protecting strength of Michael, feel him releasing your fears and strengthening your dtermination. Then feel the wisdom of Jophiel offering you clarity and confidence to continue on your journey.

- **Move across to the right of the tree to reach Netzach** or Victory. Focus on the Archangel Haniel and his power to help you feel emotionally calm and to encourage you.

- **Returning to the center of the tree you reach Tiphareth** or Beauty and the Archangel Raphael. Focus on his healing powers to restore your energy and strengthen you on the path.

- **Move upward and to the left to Geburah** or Judgment. Here Archangel Chamuel can help you focus on love and compassion in all your relationships providing a secure base from which to carry on in your journey.

- **Moving directly across you reach Chesed** or Mercy and Archangel Zadkiel. Zadkiel's energy is transformational. He can help you in your spiritual growth and help you experience the joy of alchemy.

- **Moving directly upward from Chesed** your reach Chokmah or Wisdom. Here Archangel Raziel can help you understand the secret mysteries of the universe. He is also known as the cosmic father.

- **Opposite Chokmah is Binah or Understanding.** This is ruled by Archangel Tzaphkiel, the cosmic mother. She will assist you in the contemplation of God, increasing your understanding.

- **Halfway between Binah and Chokmah you turn back downward briefly to Daath** or Knowledge. This is a non-*sephirah*, not ruled by any angel. Some Kabalists consider it as a place of miracles.

- **Directly above Daath is Kether or Crown.** This is the Divine and is ruled by the Archangel Metratron. He will assist you in reaching awareness and the highest states of bliss. You have reached the end of the journey.

- **Write down your experience** on the pages overleaf.

My tree of life meditation experience

Date _____ Time _____

I saw _____
_____
_____
_____
_____
_____

I felt _____
_____
_____
_____
_____
_____

I learned _____
_____
_____
_____
_____
_____
_____

My tree of life meditation experience

Date _____ **Time** _____

I saw _____
_____
_____
_____
_____
_____
_____

I felt _____
_____
_____
_____
_____

I learned _____
_____
_____
_____
_____
_____
_____

Sound meditation

Chanting and using sound can be an extremely powerful way of welcoming angels into your life.

The following sound meditation ritual helps you to tune into the sound waves that angels recognize.

Exercise 12 SOUND MEDITATION

- **You will need:** a singing bowl (optional).

- **Choose a time when you won't be disturbed** and you are able to relax. Sit on a comfortable cushion on the floor or on a favorite chair.

- **Focus your mind on the sacred word "Shema."** This is the Hebrew for "hear," and it also forms part of Archangel Shamael's name. Now breathe deeply without straining.

- **If you have a singing bowl,** hold the mallet against the rim and very slowly rub it around the bowl, applying an even pressure until the bowl starts to sing. Simply sit quietly if you do not have a singing bowl.

- **Repeat the following affirmation,** "Archangel Shamael, let the light of God surround me, let the light of God guide me, for the harmony of all."

- **Write down your experience** on the page opposite.

My sound meditation experience

Date _____ **Time** _____

I saw _____

_____

_____

_____

_____

_____

I felt _____

_____

_____

_____

_____

I learned _____

_____

_____

_____

_____

_____

Angel temple meditation

Every archangel has a temple of light that is anchored in the etheric realms above one of the Earth's power vortices. We may not be able to see them with the naked eye but we can visit them in meditations and in our dreams. This guided meditation enables you to see each of these temples in turn.

Exercise 13 ANGEL TEMPLE MEDITATION

- **Choose a time when you will not be disturbed** and you need not hurry. Sit in a straight-backed chair with your hands resting on your knees, palms facing upward, and your feet flat on the floor. If your feet do not comfortably reach the floor, rest them on a cushion.

- **Ground yourself** by imagining roots growing out of the soles of your feet and anchoring you to the Earth. Relax your body by focusing on your breathing.

- **Invoke Archangel Michael** to protect you during your meditation.

- **Close your eyes** and allow yourself to be transported through the astral realms until you are hovering over each temple in turn. Each time, pause for a few seconds to feel its energies and then thank the relevant angel for letting you see it.

- **Begin at Stonehenge,** over which Archangel Azrael's temple is located. Pause for a few seconds to feel its energies and thank Azrael for letting you see it. Now let yourself be taken to Archangel Cassiel's temple above Saturn. Tune in to its energies and thank Cassiel. Move on to St. Louis over which you can see Archangel Chamuel's temple.

- **Now let yourself be taken to Mount Shasta,** above which Archangel Gabriel's temple is located. When you are ready, move on to the temple of Archangel Haniel above the Himalayas. Then let yourself be transported to Lanchow and the temple of Archangel Jophiel.

- **When you are ready,** let yourself be taken to the temple of Archangel Melchizedek over Jerusalem. Then move on to the temple of Archangel Metatron over Luxor. Now allow yourself to be transported above Paradise Valley and the temple of Archangel Michael.

- **Move on to Fatima** and Archangel Raphael's temple. When you are ready, let yourself be taken to Archangel Raziel's temple over the ancient site of Lemuria in the Pacific Ocean. Then move on to Archangel Sandalphon's temple over El Chorro in Spain.

- **When you are ready,** let yourself be taken to Luxor and the location of Archangel Shamael's temple. Then move on to the ancient site of Atlantis in the Atlantic Ocean, above which Archangel Tzaphkiel's temple is located. Now let yourself be transported to Archangel Uriel's temple above the Tatra Mountains. Finally, move on to Cuba and Archangel Zadkiel's temple.

- **Finish your meditation** by grounding yourself as before and becoming aware of your breathing. Open your eyes and return to everyday reality.

- **Write down your experience** on the pages overleaf.

My angel temple meditation experience

Date _____ Time _____

I saw _____
_____
_____
_____
_____
_____

I felt _____
_____
_____
_____
_____
_____

I learned _____
_____
_____
_____
_____
_____

My angel temple meditation experience

Date _____ Time _____

I saw _____

_____

_____

_____

_____

_____

_____

I felt _____

_____

_____

_____

_____

_____

I learned _____

_____

_____

_____

_____

_____

My angel temple meditation experience

Date _____ **Time** _____

I saw _____

_____

_____

_____

_____

_____

I felt _____

_____

_____

_____

_____

_____

I learned _____

_____

_____

_____

_____

_____

_____

GUARDIAN ANGELS

Your guardian angel

Everyone has their own guardian angel that is appointed to them when they first incarnate. This angel will never leave them. Its task is to protect, guide, and strengthen the human being against the forces of evil. However, we all have free will, so we can ignore the guidance of our guardian angel if we wish. In addition, our guardian angel channels angelic light toward us, comforting and assisting us throughout our lives.

God's love is unconditional and does not demand anything in return. It is abundant and limitless, eternal and infinite. God does not judge us to see if we are worthy of being loved; every soul is equal and, because we are created in God's image, we too are Divine. Therefore we are all worthy of having a guardian angel, and it is our angel's task to open our heart and help us become the loving

Divine being that is our birthright. Your own guardian angel has been with you since the moment you incarnated in this life. It has accompanied you through all your previous births and deaths too, and will be with you in the ones still to come. Your angel will journey with you through all your incarnations, evolving as you evolve through your shared destiny. Although you may perceive your guardian angel as a separate entity, essentially it is very much a part of you. Some people believe that their guardian angel is really their higher self.

Most people experience their first contact with the angelic realms through their guardian angel. Contact with this angel is often tangible at times of immediate danger, fear, grief, illness, or despair, or at times of great joy or creative inspiration.

 ➤ Work with your angels now For a guided meditation to meet your guardian angel, turn to Exercise 14: Journey to Meet your Guardian Angel on page 130–131.

Your guiding angels

God's love finds many expressions, and this force has been described in many different ways. Angels are an expression of God's love, and throughout your life you will attract different guiding angels. Your guiding angels will change as you evolve spiritually or need to learn a different spiritual lesson. Some people have several guiding angels working with them constantly; these angels join your guardian angel in steering you toward the completion of your destiny.

Guiding angels—just like guardian angels—are unconditional and non-judgmental. They may focus on you, but they are not enamored with you because of your good actions or repulsed by your bad actions. Your angels see only the Divine light that dwells within you and understand that your true desire is for God-realization, or "enlightenment" as the Buddhists call it. Your guardian angel is usually the one you will turn to for healing, guidance, or general help. If you seek other assistance, you are better off turning to your guiding angels or archangels. Angels have direct access to the source of spiritual wisdom and

knowledge, and their consciousness (unlike ours) is not ego-driven.

Case study
Belinda's story

One day, working in meditation with Hazel's Guardian Angel spray, I had a beautiful and profound experience in my inner world. I was standing alone outside the city of Jerusalem, and there was light pouring from the city, it felt cold and frightening. I could feel myself becoming lost in it, as if I was being swallowed by a tidal wave. Just as I was drowning in a sea of gray, a gypsy caravan flew down to me and warm, strong arms lifted me into the coziest, kindest, safest place I've ever felt. I looked up into the very dark skin and powerful eyes of someone who looked like a man, but who radiated such kindness, respect, and sacredness that I knew without any doubt he was an angel. The sense of his angelic nature was profound and unmistakable. I became aware of beautiful colored and textured fabrics around me, the warmth, flickering glow, and crackling sounds of a fire in a wood-burning stove, the coziness and safety enveloped me. He didn't speak words to me, but I was aware of his loving, powerful communication. The overall feeling was immensely calm, loving, peaceful, and safe.

Work with your angels now Turn to Exercise 15: Guardian-angel Collage on pages 134–135 for guidance on creating an angel collage to help you connect with your guardian angel.

I'm not quite there yet If this exercise feels uncomfortable, turn to Exercise 9: Your Angel Vision on page 98 to more freely explore angelic presence.

Guardian angels in history

The first historical records of winged beings come from Zoroastrianism, one of the world's oldest religions. The origin of the belief that God sends a spirit to watch over each person was common in ancient Greek philosophy and was alluded to by Plato in *Phaedo* (where he discusses the nature of the afterlife and the immortality of the soul). The notion of guardian angels or angelic guides also appears in the Old Testament (Job 33:23–6 and the Book of Daniel 10:13).

A Christian theologian, Honorius Augustodunensis (died *c.*1151), was the first to state that every soul was assigned a guardian angel the moment it was put into a body. In various passages in the New Testament the doctrine of guardian angels is suggested, but the best-known angels are those that were present in all the major events in the life of Jesus, acting as God's agents on Earth. Guardian angels are often described as shepherds (they give pastoral care); they teach people the difference between good and evil, and then give strength and protection to those who listen and comply with the angels' message.

The Celts believed that we are all surrounded by spirits, as did many other pagan groups. ("Pagan" is a term used to encompass many faiths outside the Abrahamic monotheistic groups of Judaism, Christianity, and Islam.) For the Celts, their Anamchara—angel or soul-friend—was part of their daily life. Celtic angels play the role of guardians or companions, very much as the totem animal does in other shamanic traditions. The New Age movement, and interest in native cultures, has brought a huge upsurge of interest in Celtic angels, and the Anamchara takes a special interest in helping those who are evolving spiritually.

Traditional Catholic prayer

Angel of God, my guardian dear,
To whom God's love commits me here,
Ever this day/night be at my side,
To light, to guard, to rule, and guide.
Amen.

Work with your angels now Turn to Exercise 16: Celtic Angel
Meditation on page 138, for a meditation to connect with Celtic angels.

Stories of guardian angels

It is reported that on many occasions during the Second World War servicemen felt a deep connection with their guardian angel. There are accounts of angels protecting pilots: Air Chief Marshal Sir Hugh Dowding spoke about pilots who had been helped by angels during the Battle of Britain. In his retirement Dowding became actively interested in spiritualism, both as a writer and speaker, when he joined the Theosophical Society.

There are numerous stories about guardian angels and angelic intervention, and many books on the subject. In fact I featured, with the Archangel Michael, in Glennis Eckersley's *Angel at My Shoulder* (1996). This next story is fairly typical, and occurred to a friend of mine in 1998.

Case study
Near-miss
Leaving work in Nottingham very late, having ignored my instincts to leave earlier,

I felt tired and stressed and called on my guardian angel to be with me on the long drive home. Five minutes later I was involved in a crash, when a car plowed across my path at speed and hit me. I called for help, and suddenly my car was full of beautiful angelic beings;

I became totally calm as my car veered into the path of a police car. The angels just took over, steered the car, and the next minute I was parked at the side of the road having missed the police car by a centimeter. Had I hit it, I would have died. My car was perfectly parked at the side of the road—parallel-parked far better than I can do normally, and certainly after a nasty accident. The beautiful angelic guardian stayed with me until the emergency services arrived. All I sustained was whiplash.

If ever I needed conformation of angels helping in response to a call, I got it that day. The sense of peace in the car was just amazing. I also learned to follow my instincts far more and not ignore my warnings.

Planetary angels

The planets can also help you find your guardian angel. Early astrologers thought there were seven planets in our solar system—the Sun, Moon, Mercury, Venus, Mars, Jupiter, and Saturn—because these were the only planets visible to the naked eye. Each planet was assigned an archetypal being, which not only ruled that planet, but also a particular day of the week. Each planet is also associated with a particular star sign as shown in the table opposite.

The first notions of planets being guided by angels began in Spain during the Renaissance, but were heavily suppressed by the Puritans from the 16th century onward. Nevertheless, these beliefs survived, despite the oppression and persecution that were so prevalent at the time.

As telescopes became more and more sophisticated, astronomers and astrologers were better equipped to study the heavens, leading to the discovery of Uranus, Neptune, and Pluto. Each of these planets also has an angel assigned to it.

To work with your planetary angel, simply call on the angel of the planet with which you feel the greatest affinity, which rules your birth sign or is associated with the personality trait that you need at a particular moment. For example, Mars is the planet of war and rules over those born under the sign of Aries. Call on this energy when you wish to be assertive and confident.

The planets and their ruling angels

Planet	Angel	Star sign
Sun	Archangel Michael	Leo
Moon	Archangel Gabriel	Cancer
Mercury	Archangel Raphael	Gemini and Virgo
Venus	Archangel Hagiel	Taurus and Libra
Mars	Archangel Camael	Aries and Scorpio
Jupiter	Archangel Zadkiel	Sagittarius and Pisces
Saturn	Archangel Cassiel	Capricorn and Aquarius
Uranus	Archangel Uriel	Aquarius
Neptune	Archangel Asariel	Pisces
Pluto	Archangel Asariel	Scorpio

Qualities of the planets

Each planet embodies certain key concepts and energies. Here is a summary of the main associations. As you meditate consider how these concepts relate to the associated angel. Then think about the particular protection or guidance you are looking for from your guardian angel. Remember that although the planets are associated with particular star signs you do not have to be limited by this. You may feel more in tune with particular qualities regardless of the associated star sign.

The Sun The sun is associated with the father principle and represents life force, self-expression, and vitality.

The Moon As might be expected the moon embodies the mother principle and is powerfully connected with the emotions, childhood as well as the subconscious.

Mercury This planet is associated with communication and with knowledge and reasoning. Intelligence, speech, and eloquence are all characteristics associated with this planet.

Venus This is the planet associated with both love and desire. Beauty, attraction, and intimacy are all key aspects of Venus.

Mars This planet is associated with action and assertion. Energy and will are key principles.

Jupiter This is the planet governing optimism, hope, and faith. Generosity, abundance, and good fortune are associated with Jupiter.

Saturn This is the planet of strength, discipline, and wisdom. Resilience and responsibility are features of this planet's energy.

Chiron This planet is associated with healing and integration. Resolving paradoxes and dilemmas are aspects of this planet's energy.

Uranus Originality, unpredictability, and genius are all aspects of Uranus. Intuition as well as change and nonconformity form its characteristic energy.

Neptune This is the planet of inspiration and mysticism. Enlightenment and unboundedness are principal characteristics.

Pluto This is the planet associated with rebirth and renewal. Pluto is connected with death of all kind, with both endings and beginnings.

Your personal zodiac angel

The planetary angels also rule over the zodiac. The word "zodiac" literally translates as "circle of animals." Humans were charting the passage of the stars as long as 30,000 years ago. The Chaldeans (from Assyria) charted the stars as "fixed" in space, but the planets of Jupiter, Mars, Mercury, Moon, and Saturn as moving. They noted that the planets moved in front of these fixed star positions. Texts connecting astrology with the angelic realm appeared at different times, and even today new interpretations are being added.

The zodiac is split into 12 astrological signs, each of which is associated with a particular constellation. The zodiac angels can help you understand your birth sign and what it says about your personality and can prove to be powerful guardian angels. If you have your birth chart drawn up, you can also work with other angels, such as your rising-sign angel or your moon-sign angel.

Aries Although the positive aspect of Aries is this sign's confidence, energy, and enthusiasm, the negative aspect of this sign is restlessness and a lack of perseverance. Call on Archangel Camael to increase your power and strength and access his innate sense of justice to ensure all you do is for the greater good.

Taurus Call on Archangel Hagiel to help you explore new ideas and to take risks. The positive aspect of Taurus is its perseverance in the face of adversity; the negative aspect is an inability to see other points of view. Hagiel can help you do this.

Gemini The positive aspects of Gemini make you versatile and communicative. However, the negative aspects are a butterfly mind and inconsistency. Ask Archangel Raphael to strengthen your mental focus.

Cancer Ask Archangel Gabriel to help you to remember the past without clinging to it. The positive aspects of Cancer are its sensitivity and protectiveness, but its negative aspect is a tendency to be defensive.

André Beloni

Leo The positive aspects of Leo are generosity and organizational ability; its negative aspects are pride and bossiness. Call on Archangel Michael to help you express your true self.

Virgo This sign is renowned for its efficiency and analytical abilities, but its negative aspects include a tendency to worry and to fuss over petty details. Ask Archangel Raphael to help you know what is important.

Libra Libra's positive aspects include tact and skill in creating partnerships, while its negative aspects are indecision and the desire for peace at any price. Call on Archangel Hagiel to help you to stand up for yourself when necessary.

Scorpio This sign has the ability to look below the surface of things and to transform itself; but its negative attributes include suspicion and a need to take control. Ask Archangels Camael and Azrael to help you use your power wisely.

Sagittarius Call on Archangel Zadkiel when you want to master your intellect

and use it for the good of all. The positive aspects of this sign include optimism and the ability to rise to challenges; the negative aspects include exaggeration and risk-taking.

Capricorn Capricorn's positive attributes include responsibility and common sense; while its negative attributes include pessimism and negativity. Ask Archangel Asariel to enable you to help others without making a rod for your own back.

Aquarius The positive aspects of Aquarius include intellect and humanitarianism, while the negative aspects include being stubborn and dogmatic. Ask Archangels Uriel and Cassiel to help you become more flexible toward others.

Pisces Pisces' positive attributes include artistry and compassion, but its negative attributes include being too idealistic and escapist. Ask Archangels Asariel and Zadkiel to let you empathize with others without being swept away emotionally.

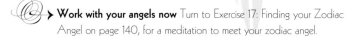 **Work with your angels now** Turn to Exercise 17: Finding your Zodiac Angel on page 140, for a meditation to meet your zodiac angel.

EXERCISES TO ATTRACT GUARDIAN ANGELS

The following exercises will help you discover your guardian angel who can offer you guidance, protection, and support.

Meeting your guardian angel

This meditation is a sacred experience, as you begin to deepen your own notion of the Divine—something far greater than yourself. It is an attunement that will enable you to open up to your angelic guardian.

 Exercise 14 JOURNEY TO MEET YOUR GUARDIAN ANGEL CD REFERENCE TRACK 5

- **Sit in a comfortable meditation posture** and relax your body by focusing on your breathing.

- **Imagine that you can breathe energy** up and down your spine, once you feel relaxed.

- **On the in-breath, move Earth energy** from the base of your spine to the crown of your head; and on the out-breath, move spiritual energy from the crown to the base. This procedure cleanses and removes any energetic blockages.

- **Bring the energy up your spine** as a thin ray of brilliant light, once you have mastered this technique and your spiritual spine feels clear. Identify yourself with this light—send it to Heaven. With it send gratitude for all the good things in your life. Imagine an overcast day as you do this. See the clouds part, as a vortex of brilliant white light comes through and settles directly above your head.

- **Absorb the light into your being** through the top of your head. This is your link with the angels.

- **Allow celestial light to pour in** through your body; feel it nurturing every cell in your body.

- **Bring in all the angelic blessings in the form of light** that are meant for you. Let this energy bathe you internally and externally.

- **Now focus your awareness on your heart center**, where the angels most strongly connect with you; visualize this gateway as rose-pink.

- **Allow your consciousness to transcend** the ordinary senses and go into a state of heightened awareness. This is your link with an unlimited realm of angelic blessings.

- **It is now time to make full contact** with your angelic guidance. From the deepest center of your heart, where your Divine spark dwells, send out your longing for an angel to be your guide—your guardian angel.

- **Feel your angel drawing closer.** Experience the change as you link in to the higher consciousness of the angelic realms.

- **Imagine, see, or feel your angel** standing beside you and enfolding you in its radiant wings of power. Experience the loving presence as your angel directs unconditional love and protection toward you.

- **You may wish to ask for guidance** or even your angel's name; be still and wait patiently for an answer.

- **To close the session**, allow your angel's presence to fade gently from view, but be assured that your angel's presence and protection will be with you as you go about your day.

- **Write down what you experienced** in the space overleaf.

My guardian-angel journey experience

Date _____ Time _____

I saw _____
_____
_____
_____
_____
_____
_____

I felt _____
_____
_____
_____
_____
_____

I learned _____
_____
_____
_____
_____
_____
_____

My guardian-angel journey experience

Date _____   Time _____

I saw _____
_____
_____
_____
_____
_____
_____

I felt _____
_____
_____
_____
_____
_____

I learned _____
_____
_____
_____
_____
_____
_____

Guardian-angel collage

You can create a collage to manifest your guardian angel and bring angelic energy into your life. The main benefit of creating this collage is to focus your mind on developing a relationship with your celestial guardian. You will see your guardian in your mind first, before you begin to see it with your spiritual eyes. Creating a collage of your guardian angel will bring it closer. You can visualize your angel in whatever form you desire. Angels can take any form—from a brilliant sphere of light to a powerful, immensely strong being, who can enfold you in its wings to protect you.

Exercise 15 GUARDIAN-ANGEL COLLAGE

- **You will need:** a stack of New Age or spiritual magazines or other visual material, other art supplies, such as glitter, feathers, or small crystals (optional), a piece
of plain paper the size of your intended collage, scissors and glue, a base for your collage.

- **Find a quiet space where you will not be disturbed.** Sit quietly for several minutes, breathe deeply and allow your heart chakra to open and blossom. Ask your guardian angel to draw close and inspire you.

- **Begin to cut out and paste down images** to which you intuitively feel attracted, on a piece of plain paper. You can paint, draw, add glitter, feathers, or crystals. People with no previous artistic ability seem to be able to draw angels! Or, if you prefer, you could write down how you instinctively feel your guardian angel looks—perhaps something like the following: "Before it appears the air shimmers, fizzes, and sparkles; it is tall, elegant, and graceful, surrounded by a golden light, wearing robes of crystalline light. It has a voice that is sonorous and resonating, a twinkle in its sparkling eyes, gleaming hair, and majestic wings. And, above all, a radiantly beautiful, loving presence."

- **Ask your guardian angel to energize the collage** when you have finished it. Then paste the collage onto a base.

- **Place your angelic collage on a wall** where you will see it, especially during your meditation.

- **Write down what you experienced** in the space overleaf.

My guardian-angel collage experience

Date _____ **Time** _____

I saw _____

_____

_____

_____

_____

_____

I felt _____

_____

_____

_____

_____

_____

I learned _____

_____

_____

_____

_____

_____

_____

My guardian-angel collage experience

Date _____   Time _____

I saw _____

_____

_____

_____

_____

_____

_____

I felt _____

_____

_____

_____

_____

_____

I learned _____

_____

_____

_____

_____

_____

_____

A Celtic guardian angel

There are many Celtic angels, including those that work on a close level with humans. This meditation connects with your own Celtic guardian angel, or Amanchara, which can take many unexpected forms.

Exercise 16 CELTIC ANGEL MEDITATION

- **Sit in a comfortable meditation posture** and allow your eyes to close.

- **Focus on your breathing,** slowing it down until you feel completely relaxed.

- **Imagine yourself in a beautiful natural setting.** Take a few moments to really feel part of it. Sit on the grass or on some other suitable surface.

- **Invite your Amanchara to draw close.** Say "Dear Amanchara, please reveal yourself to me so that I may work with you."

- **Wait for your Amanchara to appear,** in whichever form it wants to take.

- **Lovingly greet your Amanchara** and communicate with it by touch, conversation, or images.

- **When you are ready,** thank your Amanchara for meeting you and ask it to give you a sign so you will always know when it is near you.

- **Allow yourself to come back slowly,** taking your time and gently grounding yourself.

- **Write down what you experienced** in the space opposite.

My Celtic angel meditation experience

Date _____ **Time** _____

I saw _____

_____

_____

_____

_____

_____

I felt _____

_____

_____

_____

_____

I learned _____

_____

_____

_____

_____

_____

Finding your zodiac angel

The angels who love and protect you from the celestial realm are very joyous at your response to their influence and assistance. In this meditation you begin to work with these "radiant, pulsing beings of light," the zodiac angels (see pages 126–128). Zodiac angels make their presence felt by directing colored beams of light, or by surrounding you with magnificent spheres full of pulsing, kaleidoscopic, sacred-geometric, vibrant light.

 Exercise 17 FINDING YOUR ZODIAC ANGEL
CD REFERENCE TRACK 6

- **You will need:** a yoga mat or futon, a pillow, a light blanket.

- **Stretch out on your back,** using a yoga mat or futon on the floor, somewhere you will not be disturbed. Place a pillow under your knees and cover yourself with a light blanket. Let your arms relax, palms up and at your side. Keep your heels slightly apart.

- **Listen to the sound of my voice** and breathe slowly and deeply, feeling a sense of deep calm come over your whole body. You feel safe, protected, and very relaxed. You are now ready to meet your zodiac angel.

- **Magnificent spheres** of pulsing, kaleidoscopic, brilliant-colored lights of varying sizes begin to form around you: beautiful magenta, emerald-green, moonlight-silver, vibrant red, warm orange, sunshine-yellow, sapphire-blue, violet, rose-pink, indigo, turquoise, and jade-green.

- **The colored spheres move around you** and through you, bathing your body, mind, and spirit with angelic energy. You feel happy and relaxed, calm and peaceful. Each of the 12 spheres is an angel of the zodiac.

- **You become very aware** of one of the colored spheres as it begins to merge with you totally: its mind becomes your mind, its heart becomes your heart, its consciousness becomes your consciousness. This angelic being is your zodiac angel.

- **Experience its unconditional love,** protection, and healing.

- **You may wish to ask for guidance** or your zodiac angel's name; be still and wait patiently for the answer. It is now time for your zodiac angel and the other angels to leave.

- **To close the session** let your zodiac angel's presence gently fade from view. Rest assured that your angel's presence and protection will be with you as you go about your day.

- **Write down what you experienced** in the space overleaf.

My zodiac-angel experience

Date _____ **Time** _____

I saw _____
_____
_____
_____
_____
_____

I felt _____
_____
_____
_____
_____
_____

I learned _____
_____
_____
_____
_____
_____

My zodiac-angel experience

Date _____ Time _____

I saw _____
_____
_____
_____
_____
_____
_____

I felt _____
_____
_____
_____
_____
_____

I learned _____
_____
_____
_____
_____
_____
_____

My zodiac-angel experience

Date _____ **Time** _____

I saw _____

_____

_____

_____

_____

_____

I felt _____

_____

_____

_____

_____

_____

I learned _____

_____

_____

_____

_____

_____

_____

ANGEL HEALING

How angels can heal

Angelic healing and other mystical experiences are not some New Age fad. The stories of unexplained rescues by angels who have appeared in times of need have been well documented throughout history. I have questioned hundreds of people who have had angelic sightings, including beyond-the-veil (or near-death) experiences and the evolution of consciousness that serious trauma and injury can bring about, unfolding someone's psychic abilities.

Case study
Near-death experience

Angels are the only creation that transcend both the earthly side and the other side. My friend June has seen angels since she was a little girl; in fact June and I are the same: lifelong clairvoyants, mediums, teachers, and therapists. June's story provides not only a description of angelic healing, but proof of life after death. On March 1 2001, June was involved in a head-on fatal car accident.

Without warning, a car plowed straight into hers, and the person driving the other car died. The first thing June saw after the impact, when the air went still, was a beautiful angel, with long, blond hair, clothed in white robes—larger than a normal person—with huge wings that were glowing in a brilliant golden mist. The angel took her to a garden that was full of magical colors (Paradise). June saw in the distance people she knew and asked the angel: could she go and join them—could she stay here? The angel said no, she had to go back, as she still had much work to do. The angel told her to remember the garden and teach people to use these heavenly angelic colors to heal. Of course, June was in no pain when she was with the angel, but the moment she was back in her body, and in the three long months that she was in hospital and during the many operations she underwent, June used the memory of that garden and the heavenly colors to ease her pain. In her healing practice June sends these colors to people as glowing orbs of scintillating light.

Physical healing

Archangel Raphael is the angel to call on whenever physical healing is needed. His name means "God has healed" and it is his task to help anyone who is in need of medical help. He is often depicted holding a bowl of healing lotion, and with a caduceus in one hand. Although he rules over the heart chakra, he will send healing to any part of the body.

You can ask Archangel Raphael to heal you whenever you are ill, or you can ask him to send healing to someone else. When you need healing for yourself, you can do it by asking out loud for healing, thinking it, or even writing him a letter. Choose whichever method seems most appropriate to you at the time. After you have invoked Raphael's help, be open to the thoughts and images that come to you. He may be sending you suggestions about how to improve your health or which remedies will make you feel better, or he might connect with you in your dreams. He may also tell you to summon immediate medical aid if you have not already done so. He works in conjunction with doctors and nurses, even if they are not aware of his presence, so there is no need to worry about a conflict of interests.

If you want to ask Raphael to send healing to someone you care about, he will go to their aid but he cannot interfere in their free will. Even if there are reasons why he cannot physically heal someone, he will bring them comfort and do whatever he can to make them feel better. Trust that everything is working out in the way that God intends, and behave in a calm, peaceful, and loving manner that improves the situation for everyone involved. You can also call on Archangel Raphael to guide you when selecting remedies, such as aromatherapy oils, crystals, and flower essences, whether these are for you or for someone else.

If you want to know whether Raphael has heard your request for healing, look out for unusual activity from birds, such as a bird staring at you or tapping on the window. You might also see a white feather in a place where you would not normally expect to find it.

 **Work with your angels now** For a visualization to meet Archangel Raphael, turn to Exercise 18: Healing Meditation on page 162.

Emotional healing

The Archangel Chamuel and the angels of love help you to renew and improve your relationships with others by assisting you in developing your heart chakra. Many people are afraid of opening their heart chakra. Those who have been able to overcome this fear have charismatic warmth that others find reassuring. Archangel Chamuel can help you in all your relationships, and especially through life-changing situations such as conflict, divorce, bereavement, and even job loss. Always ask Archangel Chamuel to assist you in opening your heart chakra, to develop your healing gifts as well as your angelic communication.

Many people search for a soulmate and seek the assistance of Archangel Chamuel. A soulmate is someone you meet and with whom you have a deep and natural affinity—a rapport and a sense of familiarity. There is no doubt that a soulmate will help you awaken your heart center, for soulmates are friends, relatives, and loved ones who are responsive to your love, and with whom you feel deeply connected, usually sharing a common path. A soulmate may be deeply connected to you from your previous lives, and you may already have several soulmates. I personally have several dear friends whom I consider soulmates and I have journeyed with them through many lifetimes. If you wish to attract a soulmate, you need to let go of the illusion that there is a perfect person just waiting for you who will fulfill your every expectation. If you sincerely want a soulmate, ask the Archangel Chamuel to assist you.

Case study
Finding a soulmate
I had met someone who seemed perfect for me. I had asked the angels to help me, but I still needed proof, and that night I was awakened by a beautiful angel who smiled at me, and I felt it was saying that I had chosen the right person. That was forty years ago, and we are still happily married.

 Work with your angels now To work with the Archangel Chamuel, turn to Exercise 19: Loving Meditation on pages 164–165.

I'm not quite there yet If you feel emotionally blocked turn to Exercise 5: Chakra Awareness Visualization on pages 66–67 to get better in touch with your emotions.

Spiritual healing

Angels respect our free will, and they will never challenge our right to make our own choices, but they may challenge our outworn patterns and belief systems. Sometimes we need to rethink the meaning of our lives, to become unstuck and clear dysfunctional emotional baggage, which causes subconscious programming that needs to be removed so that we can move forward confidently in life. Such programming often develops within the illusion of self-defense against painful experiences and unbalanced relationships.

Zadkiel's angelic mission of mercy is to unchain us from the heavy burden of unhealed energy, so that we can reclaim the freedom to flourish. Invoke the Archangel Zadkiel and visualize yourself in a violet flame, then place your troubles and difficult relationships within the flame so that all negativity is transmuted. Forgiveness is not always easy: when you are angry, you blame, resent, and hate. These feelings do not go away just by themselves, and you need to ask for the gift of forgiveness by calling on Archangel Zadkiel and the violet flame of freedom. It contains the Holy Spirit's power to transmute the cause—negativity, sin, and negative karma.

Case study
Transformation

I suffered severe painful abuse as a child, bullying during my school years, and physical and mental abuse in previous relationships, when there was no one in my family to support me. I asked God for help, and he sent Archangel Zadkiel to help me realize that I had a choice in which pathway I would walk. I could play the victim for the rest of my life, thereby allowing my abusers to control me long after the event, or I could ask for transformation and take charge of my own destiny and change my life's path.

 **Work with your angels now** To work with the Archangel Zadkiel, turn to Exercise 20: Spiritual Growth Meditation on pages 168–169 for a spiritual healing exercise.

Distant healing

Some of the original sacred sources on Sandalphon refer to him as the prophet Elijah, transfigured and raised to angelic status. Other sources describe him as the "twin brother" of Metatron, whose human origin as Enoch was similar to the human origin of Sandalphon. He is uniformly depicted as extremely tall, uniting Heaven and Earth. He is credited with gathering the prayers of the faithful, weaving them into a wreath and delivering them to God. Sandalphon is also known as the angel of the Earth, and so assists in sending distant healing.

We can request that remote, transformational, angelic healing be directed to the needy, the desperate, the grieving, and the bereaved, to all those on the face of the Earth who are afraid or suffering. Whatever the disaster—man-made or natural, famine-stricken or war-torn—Sandalphon and his angels are awaiting our summons. Of course we can also send this angelic help to our family,

friends, and anyone we know who is in need of angelic assistance.

Distant healing can be achieved in several different ways. The easiest is by a simple unconditional prayer for the person or situation you wish to help. The next way is to form an angelic energy sphere. Focus your intent on where you want the orb to go, then summon the angels and imagine, feel, or visualize the sphere forming between your hands. Archangel Sandalphon normally works with a mixture of rainbow colors: red, orange, yellow, green, blue, indigo, and violet. If you feel that pink, turquoise, or some other color is needed, then Sandalphon will assist you and will energize and then deliver a pulsing orb of healing light.

It is always a good idea to get permission to do distant healing on someone. If this is not possible, then direct that the energy be used for the highest good of all and to harm none.

 **Work with your angels now** To work with the Archangel Sandalphon, turn to Exercise 21: Planetary Healing Meditation on pages 172–173.

Dream healing

Tzaphkiel is the archangel of deep contemplation of God, representing the nurturing, Divine-feminine watery aspect of creation. Tzaphkiel gives us glimpses of alternate realities, and will catch us if we fall or falter—for the feminine aspect of God's infinite love is unconditional. On the Kabalistic tree of life, Tzaphkiel is the "Cosmic Mother" who rules over Binah (understanding); in Binah, true understanding comes from limitations and struggle—it is where we heed the lessons of time and patience. "Pain is a prod to remembrance," according to Paramahansa Yogananda, the early 20th-century Indian guru.

Tzaphkiel teaches us what we must relinquish in order to gain full understanding of our immortal soul. He is associated with the primal waters where all sparks of life are created, and therefore this angelic energy is never normally summoned; however, when requested respectfully, it will work with us through vivid dreams.

Case study
Angelic dream

I had an amazing dream of you last night. The colors were wonderful; it became a vision of a raven, the color of labradorite, holding on to a branch with its right claw and holding an amethyst in its left claw whilst it was looking to its left. Just below, on another branch, was a large horned owl holding a moonstone in its right claw and looking to its right. Behind them both, through the leaves, was a long waterfall of a brilliant enamel-blue falling into a lake reflecting a star-filled midnight sky. The waterfall came from in between a pair of pure, pearlized angel wings, the bottom feathers touching the edge of the lake, which was far below and had a pine forest to the right below the raven, and beautiful rocks on the other side below the owl. The air was so pure and crisp. It was beyond mortal words, and I didn't want to return. I may find out what it was about one day.

 **Work with your angels now** To discover how to incubate a healing dream with an angelic crystal, turn to Exercise 22: Incubating a Healing Dream on pages 175–176.

Guidance

Archangel Gabriel is the heavenly messenger of God, who awakens your "inner angel" and transforms your mind to receive Gabriel's healing gifts of hope, happiness, love, angelic guidance, and etheric celestial wings. Gabriel is the archangel to summon to dissolve fear and guide you through life changes.

He is found in the sacred texts of all religions, and it is said that Gabriel will be the angel who will blow the trumpet that initiates the end-times and the general resurrection at the "Last Judgment." Gabriel's shining light of perfect protection steers you through difficult moments and keeps all your loved ones safe, providing guidance, clarity, vision, and discipline to follow your path.

The Archangel Gabriel always reminds us to ask the angels for what we need. The angel said, "Ask, ask, ask, for all you need, for we love to assist you and to give you gifts; ask sincerely and thankfully, for we delight in our interaction with you."

Case study
Requesting help

Martyne was desperate to find other employment; she had to work long hours and most weekends too, and she never seemed to get any quality time with her husband and young son. She'd applied for dozens of jobs, and had attended a few interviews, which were unfortunately unsuccessful. She was beginning to give up hope. Finally her husband said to her, "Have you written to the angels?" Somehow she had been so despondent and unhappy that she had forgotten that the angels need us to ask them for assistance. Within two days she was offered one of the jobs that she had been interviewed for, and she was ecstatic. Two days after that she was offered another one of the jobs she had been interviewed for. So now she had a choice. Martyne wanted me to include her story as a reminder to you to ask the angels.

Relationships

Uriel is the archangel for emotional harmony and mental clarity. He saves us from confusion and bestows inner peace. When you are going through turbulent life changes, ask the Archangel Uriel to smooth your path. Let him assist you in keeping cool, calm, and collected, especially when things around you are going crazy. For instance, if you have financial problems or feel that relationships are falling apart, Uriel can help you think straight. If you are having trouble with authority figures, bosses, co-workers, or customers, ask Uriel to guide you. He works in ways that will astound you.

Uriel can help you deal with inner conflict, trouble sleeping, anger, or volatile personal relationships. Whenever feelings of stress or agitation build up, ask Archangel Uriel to clear the energy from your solar-plexus chakra. Uriel helps heal every aspect of life, turning disappointment into success, finding blessings in misfortune as well as bringing harmony to chaotic situations. He asks us to aspire to oneness with all humanity, releasing the painful memories and burdens of the past by applying unconditional forgiveness.

Case study
Angelic peace

My personal visions of Archangel Uriel have always been supportive, especially when I have been beset by a multitude of obstacles and when the tasks I have been given are overwhelming and I can't, with my logical mind, find a solution. He appears—vast white feather wings, dark hair, dark eyes aflame with the light of God. He commands respect by his very presence and peaceful disposition. He always reminds me to "let go and let God"—and as soon as I surrender, all obstacles vanish as the mere illusion they are, and I am able once more to fulfill my Dharma.

EXERCISES FOR ANGEL HEALING

The following exercises will help you access the extraordinary
healing power of angels.

Channeling angel healing

The emerald-green ray of the Archangel Raphael has healing as its focus. His "temple of light" or ashram is over Fatima, in Portugal (see pages 94–96 for a list of the other archangels' temple locations and colors). Raphael brings healing, harmony, and balance for body, mind, spirit, and soul.

Exercise 18 HEALING MEDITATION

- **Sit in a comfortable meditation posture,** letting the chair beneath you take the full weight of your body, and relax.

- **Close your eyes** and relax your body even more, by focusing on your breathing; let it become slower and deeper, with the out-breath being slower than the in-breath.

- **Summon the Archangel Raphael,** whose ashram you wish to visit, and ask for your conscious awareness to be transported there during the meditation.

- **Use the following invocation:** "Archangel Raphael, guide me as I release all dis-ease. I now choose a healthy body, mind, and spirit. I am instantly transformed. I ask under the law of Divine grace, Amen."

- **Feel Archangel Raphael drawing closer;** let yourself be surrounded by a sphere of emerald-green healing energy and gently transported to his "spiritual home" above Fatima, Portugal.

- **State that you require healing** when you reach the ashram.

- **When it is time to return from your meditation,** Archangel Raphael will bring you safely back to your body and place you gently in the chair.

- **Give thanks** and, in your own time, open your eyes.

- **Write down what you experienced** in the space opposite.

My healing meditation experience

Date _____ **Time** _____

I saw _____

_____

_____

_____

_____

_____

I felt _____

_____

_____

_____

_____

I learned _____

_____

_____

_____

_____

_____

Channeling loving energy

Archangel Chamuel rules the pink ray of unconditional love. His "temple of light" or ashram is situated over St. Louis, Missouri, in the United States (see pages 94–96 for a list of the other archangels' temple locations and colors). Chamuel opens the heart chakra to improve relationships and create partnership harmony and understanding.

 ## Exercise 19 LOVING MEDITATION
CD REFERENCE TRACK 7

- **Sit in a comfortable meditation posture,** letting the chair beneath you take the full weight of your body, and relax.

- **Close your eyes** and listen to the sound of my voice.

- **Relax your body even more** by focusing on your breathing; let it become slower and deeper, with the out-breath being slower than the in-breath.

- **Summon the Archangel Chamuel,** whose ashram you want to visit, and ask for your conscious awareness to be transported there during the meditation.

- **Use the following invocation:** "Archangel Chamuel, guide me toward happy and satisfying relationships. Help me to show unconditional love to others and to receive their love in return. Let me be free of all self-interest in my relationships. Help me to attract soulmates into my life now. Thank you for your love and guidance. Amen."

- **Feel Archangel Chamuel drawing closer;** let yourself be surrounded by a sphere of loving pink energy and gently transported to his temple of light above St. Louis, Missouri.

- **When you reach his ashram,** say that you want to be helped to create happy and fulfilling relationships. Be receptive to the energies that flow toward you.

- **When it is time to return from your meditation,** Archangel Chamuel will bring you safely back to your body and place you gently in your chair.

- **Give thanks** and, in your own time, open your eyes.

- **Write down what you experienced** in the space overleaf.

My loving meditation experience

Date _____ **Time** _____

I saw _____

_____

_____

_____

_____

_____

_____

I felt _____

_____

_____

_____

_____

_____

_____

I learned _____

_____

_____

_____

_____

_____

_____

My loving meditation experience

Date _____ **Time** _____

I saw _____
_____
_____
_____
_____
_____

I felt _____
_____
_____
_____
_____
_____

I learned _____
_____
_____
_____
_____
_____
_____

Channeling spiritual healing

Archangel Zadkiel rules the violet ray of self-transformation and spiritual growth. His "temple of light" or ashram is situated over Cuba (see pages 94–96 for a list of the other archangels' temple locations and colors). Zadkiel opens the crown chakra to create insight and spiritual growth.

Exercise 20 SPIRITUAL GROWTH MEDITATION

- **Sit in a comfortable meditation posture,** letting the chair beneath you take the full weight of your body, and relax.

- **Allow your eyes to close.**

- **Relax your body even more** by focusing on your breathing; let it become slower and deeper, with the out-breath being slower than the in-breath.

- **Summon the Archangel Zadkiel,** whose ashram you want to visit, and ask for your conscious awareness to be transported there during the meditation.

- **Use the following invocation:** "Archangel Zadkiel, help me to gain greater insight into myself so that I may release all the habits, actions, and thoughts that hold me back from expressing my positive energy. Please give me the courage to transform myself and to connect with my Divine self. Thank you for your love and guidance. Amen."

- **Feel Archangel Zadkiel drawing closer;** let yourself be surrounded by a sphere of loving violet energy and gently transported to his temple above Cuba.

- **When you reach his ashram,** state that you want to be helped to transform yourself and to know cosmic freedom. Be receptive to the energies that flow toward you.

- **When it is time to return from your meditation,** Archangel Zadkiel will bring you safely back to your body and place you gently in your chair.

- **Give thanks** and, in your own time, open your eyes.

- **Write down what you experienced** in the space overleaf.

My spiritual growth meditation experience

Date _____ **Time** _____

I saw _____
_____
_____
_____
_____
_____

I felt _____
_____
_____
_____
_____
_____

I learned _____
_____
_____
_____
_____
_____
_____

My spiritual growth meditation experience

Date _____ Time _____

I saw _____
_____
_____
_____
_____
_____

I felt _____
_____
_____
_____
_____
_____

I learned _____
_____
_____
_____
_____
_____

Channeling planetary healing

Archangel Sandalphon is the angel responsible for the welfare of all mankind and is the guardian of the Earth. His "temple of light" or ashram is situated over El Chorro in Spain (see pages 94–96 for a list of the other archangels' temple locations and colors). Archangel Sandalphon is represented by all the colors of the rainbow.

Exercise 21 PLANETARY HEALING MEDITATION

- **Sit in a comfortable meditation posture,** letting the chair beneath you take the full weight of your body, and relax.

- **Allow your eyes to close.**

- **Relax your body even more** by focusing on your breathing; let it become slower and deeper, with the out-breath being slower than the in-breath.

- **Summon the Archangel Sandalphon,** whose ashram you want to visit, and ask for your conscious awareness to be transported there during the meditation.

- **Use the following invocation:** "Archangel Sandalphon, help me to send out healing to all mankind, so that I may be of assistance to anyone in need. Guide me so I can become a force for good. Help me to send love and light to everyone and to send loving energy to our beloved planet. Thank you for being with me. Amen."

- **Feel Archangel Sandalphon drawing closer;** let yourself be surrounded by a sphere of loving rainbow energy and gently transported to his temple above El Chorro in Spain.

- **When you reach his ashram,** state that you want to be helped to transform yourself and to know cosmic freedom. Be receptive to the energies that flow toward you.

- **When it is time to return from your meditation,** Archangel Sandalphon will bring you safely back to your body and place you gently in your chair.

- **Give thanks** and, in your own time, open your eyes.

- **Write down what you experienced** in the space overleaf.

My planetary healing meditation experience

Date _____ **Time** _____

I saw _____

_____

_____

_____

_____

_____

I felt _____

_____

_____

_____

_____

I learned _____

_____

_____

_____

_____

_____

Incubating a healing dream

One of the easiest ways of connecting with angels for healing is through dreams. Many crystals are defined as "dream" crystals, and placing one of these under your pillow will help incubate the energy of angelic healing. During the night, while you sleep, your spiritual aspect may take over, and you may find that you wake up holding your dream crystal in your hand.

You can choose any of the angelic crystals described on pages 58–64. I would personally suggest angel-aura quartz™, which clears the mind for finer levels of communication. It is linked to the crown chakra, so it will energize all the subtle-energy systems for the broadest spectrum of healing. It also embodies a magnificent harmony that draws the angels.

Exercise 22 INCUBATING A HEALING DREAM

- **You will need**: an angelic crystal (see pages 58–64)
- **Start by taking some slow, deep breaths,** making the out-breath slower than the in-breath. Imagine that you are breathing in the energies of your crystal, when your intuition tells you—breathe into the crystal your intent to receive healing.
- **Invoke the Archangel Tzaphkiel** to assist you in your healing dream.
- **Place the crystal under your pillow** before you go to sleep.
- **Gently remind yourself** that on waking you will remember your angelic dream.
- **Note down what you remember of your dream** as soon as possible after waking. Keeping an angel-experience journal will help you work with your dreams and open the gateway to angel healing.
- **Write down what you experienced** in the space overleaf.

My healing-dream incubation experience

Date _____ Time _____

I saw _____

_____

_____

_____

_____

_____

I felt _____

_____

_____

_____

_____

I learned _____

_____

_____

_____

_____

_____

ANGELS OF ASSISTANCE

Angelic intervention

Angels are always waiting for you to ask for their assistance. They are not allowed to interfere in your free will, so they cannot intercede on your behalf unless requested to do so. But once you ask them for help, they will do all they can to assist, provided that what you have asked for will not harm anyone and is for the greater good of everyone concerned. So how do you ask angels for help?

There are many different methods, depending on what feels right for you and is suitable at that moment. For instance, when you have plenty of spare time you could contact your chosen angel in a peaceful and relaxed meditation. But when your child is ill and you are frantically waiting for the doctor to arrive, you might quickly ask for their help out loud or by sending them a silent prayer. There is no need to worry about the angels being offended by your urgent cry for help. They will still come to your aid.

Of course, they will like it if you show your appreciation by thanking them when you ask for their help and also when you receive it. These are your lifelong friends and as you begin to establish a relationship with them you will find that you instinctively welcome them and thank them for their help. You will also feel it when they draw near.

Each angel can help you in a particular way, as you will discover in the following pages. For instance, Haziel gives you courage and strength, while Muriel will help in times of emotional turmoil. But if you cannot remember which angel to call on, there is no cause for worry. Simply send out your message, confident that the angel you need will hear your request and come to your aid.

> **Work with your angels now** Turn to Exercise 23: Angel Affirmation on page 194 to ask the angels to help you achieve your goals, and Exercise 24: Ritual for Promoting Spiritual Growth on page 196 for a ritual to raise your consciousness.

Assistance in times of weakness

Archangel Haniel, whose name means "glory of God," is the angel to call on whenever you need mental, emotional, spiritual, or physical strength. He will help you to connect with your soul's mission, so that you can be confident of being on the right path and of achieving the goals that your soul chose before it incarnated into your present lifetime. With his help, you can fully develop your individuality without fear.

Haniel rules the turquoise ray of self-expression through the emotions. This influences the higher heart chakra, known as the thymus chakra. With his help, you can let your soul expand and become free from the constraints that others place on it. He will sharpen and refine your perception so you can see your life clearly, and so you can enjoy a deeper and more life-enhancing connection with God.

Invoke Archangel Haniel whenever you need the inner strength to carry on, when life's problems have got the better of you or when you feel unsettled. Ask him to protect and support you, and to give you the determination to achieve your life's purpose.

Physical associations Haniel helps to relieve sore throats, asthma and other respiratory conditions, diabetes, nervous tension, headaches, and dizziness. He also helps to reduce allergies and boosts depleted immune systems.

Emotional and mental associations Haniel fosters a sense of calm by quelling nervous tension and establishing a feeling of peace; he brings turbulent emotions back into balance; creates inner confidence; boosts inner strength; strengthens moral courage.

Spiritual associations Haniel gives you the strength to overcome difficulties and combat negativity; he enhances communication with your angels and spirit guides; he heightens your intuition and your sixth sense.

> **Work with your angels now** For a meditation to seek Archangel Haniel's help, turn to Exercise 25: Meditation for Angelic Assistance on page 200.

Emotional assistance

Archangel Muriel, whose name means "angel of the sea," is the angel to connect with when you need help in coping with your turbulent emotions. She will support you so you do not feel alone, and she will help you to gain mastery of your emotions. Her nurturing energy brings peace and tranquility, quietening troubled emotions and balancing mood swings.

Because of her connection with the sea, Muriel is associated with the color aquamarine. She is also the guardian angel of the zodiac sign Cancer and she governs the month of June in which the sign of Cancer begins. Muriel has a connection with all marine life but is particularly associated with dolphins and whales.

Invoke Archangel Muriel whenever you need to get in touch with your feelings so you can understand them better or discover what they are telling you, and honor them. Allow Muriel to help you gain insight and understanding of the needs of the people around you as well.

Physical associations Muriel helps to control the amount of fluid in the human body, so can assist in treating water retention; she is also the angel to call on for women's reproductive problems, such as fibroids, irregular menstruation, endometriosis, and the menopause.

Emotional and mental associations Muriel assists when emotional turbulence and confusion interfere with objectivity and reasoning; helps us to appreciate the emotional viewpoints of others; soothes feelings of panic, helplessness, and victimization; counteracts defensiveness, mood swings, and insecurity; fosters a loving, supportive energy.

Spiritual associations Muriel enhances empathy and compassion; has a grounding effect; brings emotional stability; combats dreaminess and otherworldliness; increases psychic sensitivity; enhances and encourages the ability to sense subtle energies.

 → **Work with your angels now** For meditation to seek Archangel Muriel's assistance, turn to Exercise 26: In Times of Trouble Meditation on page 204.

Assistance in finding your destiny

Archangel Auriel, whose name means "light of God," is the feminine aspect of Archangel Uriel. Like him, she will help you to discover your destiny and your true path in life. Auriel is known as the "lunar angel" because she works exclusively through the mysterious energies of the moon. Her color is silver, like the moon's face.

In the Kabalistic system, Auriel and Uriel rule over the *sephirah* of Malkuth, which represents the kingdom of God.

Invoke Archangel Auriel whenever you want to know and understand your destiny in life. Ask her to help you gain insight into your life's calling and the choices you are making. Call on Auriel to illuminate your path when you are unsure of the direction in which you are heading and you need angelic guidance to set you back on track or when you want to aim for new horizons. Work with Auriel's lunar energies by connecting with her at the time of the full moon each month, when your psychic power is enhanced.

Physical associations Auriel assists in childbirth, creating a peaceful environment for the birth. She also helps mothers to feed their babies, to wean them, and to feed their children. She combats insomnia and nightmares, leading to peaceful and restful sleep.

Emotional and mental associations Auriel harmonizes the female aspect of your personality, helping to balance it with your male side. She helps to regulate depression and fluctuating moods, and calms repetitive thoughts. She assists in lucid dreaming and in analyzing dreams.

Spiritual associations Auriel allows a spiritual connection with your subconscious, so you can probe its depths and release your fears. She helps you to understand the twists and turns your life has taken. She enhances your natural psychic gifts and your intuition.

Assistance in clairvoyance

Archangel Raziel, whose name means "the secret of God," rules the indigo ray of insight and intuition. This influences the third-eye chakra, thereby giving us an inner vision and hidden knowledge. Sacred texts tell us that Raziel proclaims the secrets of men each day on Mount Horeb. With his assistance, you can boost your clairaudience, clairvoyance, clairsentience, and claircognizance, so you can know things without being told and you can create stronger communication with your angels.

In the Kabalistic system, Raziel rules over the *sephirah* of Chokmah, which represents the active wisdom of God. Raziel's gifts include understanding, insight,connections with spirit, and the ability to tune into Divine guidance and the secrets of the universe.

Invoke Archangel Raziel whenever you want to connect with the world of spirit and enhance your intuition. Ask him to help you gain more insight into your life and to help you to see more clearly during your angelic meditations and visualizations. Let him open your ears to the messages of the angels so you can fully understand them. Ask him to protect you from negative energies and to keep your own energies pure and radiant at all times.

Physical associations Raziel soothes sinus and bronchial complaints; reduces insomnia, migraine, and tension headaches; lowers high blood pressure; eases back pain, sciatica, and lumbago; balances overactive thyroid conditions; reduces physical pain, kills bacteria, and clears all forms of pollution.

Emotional and mental associations Raziel helps to reduce the power of obsessions and to create a balanced mental outlook; he steadies emotional turmoil; he increases your self-awareness and ability to understand yourself.

Spiritual associations Raziel enhances telepathy, intuition, precognition, and all other forms of psychic knowledge; he clears negative thought forms and purifies atmospheres; he deepens spiritual and psychic understanding.

Finding other Earth angels

Angel workshops, courses, and seminars are available worldwide and online. I have taught angel seminars around the world since 1990, and I also run distance courses on the angel essences that I have created, called "Archangel Enlightenment." I know that today many people feel drawn to find other Earth angels. They feel inspired to help others attune to the angelic realms. Several of my dearest friends run angel courses, and it seems that the Earth-angel network is spreading like wildfire. Archangel Michael rules over the element of fire, and it is his guidance that is bringing about this energy expansion, which is designed to excite, inspire, and inflame the hearts of spiritual seekers to become "light-workers."

You may have friends who are also drawn to the angelic realm. I know someone who has formed a local angel group.

They meet every month on the same day, so that people remember it. They take turns to use each other's houses, and the host provides the drinks, but group members all bring a small gift of food to share, or candles and flowers as offerings to the angels. They often give each other angel readings, or review new angel books, CDs, and angel cards, and swap angel stories. They also take it in turns to give a guided meditation, and end their gatherings by working as a group to send absent healing to those in need. Occasionally they have a guest speaker.

You do not have to live close to other Earth angels because there are many Internet groups out there. So no one ever needs to feel isolated; in fact there is never any lack of support. Ask your angels to guide you to find other Earth angels.

Work with your angels now Turn to Exercise 27: Earth Angels Group Meditation page 207 for a guided meditation.

Angelic humans

Angelic humans: this is a fascinating subject and one that divides people who "believe in angels." Many people believe that human and angelic evolution run in parallel. However, there is a branch of extra-canonical writings that is rich in angelic lore: the three Books of Enoch. In 1 Enoch 70, "The Final Translation of Enoch," we see Enoch transformed into the Archangel Metatron. There is also an ancient tradition that the Archangel Sandalphon once took human form as the prophet Elijah. The Swedish scientist, philosopher, and mystic Emanuel Swedenborg (1688–1772) believed that angels were perfected humans, much like Buddhist bodhisattvas.

Some people believe that the angelic human race was created to act as planetary stewards of the Earth's sacred evolution. During this time of transformation and change, angelic humans are awakening from their deep sleep and remembering. Angelic humans are very sensitive souls with natural empathic abilities.

Angelic humans have great inner light and extraordinary spiritual abilities. These incarnate souls have a powerful resonance of Divine energy and usually act as channels for the "spiritual hierarchy" of angels, archangels, and Ascended Masters (spiritually enlightened beings who in past incarnations were ordinary humans).

Some of these angelic humans are conscious of their original angel origins and realize they were created by the Divine to hold the Christ-consciousness as part of the evolutionary plan. It is said that there are more angelic humans incarnate now than there have ever been before, and all of them are ready to receive and hold the Christ-consciousness.

Angel letters

When you have problems, you can write to your angels. Open your heart—do not hold back your thoughts, but let your feelings pour into the letter. Let go and ask the angels to resolve the problem for your highest good and the good of all. Do not try to manipulate the situation. You may be pleasantly surprised at the speed with which the problem is resolved, often in an unexpected way. Angels work in ways that you would never even dream of.

A simple way to purify your thoughts is to write down all your concerns, listing everything that makes you angry or that causes you to behave in an unangelic way. Don't hold anything back—just keep writing; tell your angels what makes you fearful, disillusioned, or disappointed. Emotions have a great effect on healing and health; when we relive negative emotions, it causes a reaction that is perceived clairvoyantly as dark areas or holes in the aura.

You could also write to someone who has upset you or caused you pain. Since you are going to burn the letter after you have written it, there is no point in keeping anything back. The process is a deliberate act of personal empowerment, which will elevate your consciousness.

When you have finished writing, do not read what you have written. Burn the piece of paper. As you do so, feel the cleansing effect this has on your body, mind, and spirit.

EXERCISES TO SUMMON ANGEL ASSISTANCE

The following exercises will help bring powerful angels of
assistance to you at times of doubt and fear.

Angel affirmation

You can reinforce your angelic connection by asking angels to help you achieve your goals, motivating you to make your dreams come true. You may be surprised, however, at how dramatically different your wishes become, once your consciousness merges with the angelic stream of love and light. How you think determines your reality. Negative thinking blights your life—it is bad for your health, your relationships, and your spiritual life. Summon the angels to help you in reprogramming your consciousness by forming a positive affirmation.

Exercise 23 ANGEL AFFIRMATION

- **You will need:** a candle, a clear quartz crystal or angel box (any box that you dedicate to angelic work).

- **Sit on a cushion or chair** in your meditation space. Light a candle and place it on your altar, if you have one.

- **Invite the angels to join you** in this creation of an affirmation.

- **Write out a positive affirmation for yourself.** Make it powerful and as appropriate as possible to your own situation. Keep all your statements positive, and for the highest good of all. My favorite personal affirmation is: "In blissful unification, my angels guide me daily."

- **Imagine or feel the affirmation has already happened** as you say it.

- **Keep your affirmation** on your altar under a clear quartz crystal or in an angel box.

- **Write down what you experienced** in the space opposite.

My angel affirmation experience

Date _____ **Time** _____

I saw _____

_____

_____

_____

_____

_____

I felt _____

_____

_____

_____

_____

I learned _____

_____

_____

_____

_____

_____

Promoting spiritual growth

This ritual is designed to raise your consciousness in order to increase your awareness of angels. The most important thing to remember is that it is the *intent* behind the ritual that provides the power. Before beginning, relax your mind and let your thoughts come and go as they please; they will slow down after a couple of minutes. This ritual creates an amulet that generates a powerful energy field around you when you wear, carry, or sleep with it; it seals and protects your aura.

Choose a Monday, the day dedicated to the moon, on which to work this angelic ritual. Choose a time when the moon is waxing, or growing larger, since this favors spells for growth (you are looking to grow spiritually and increase your protection).

The ritual should ideally be performed outdoors; however, if you choose to do it indoors, make sure you can see the moon through an open window.

Exercise 24 RITUAL FOR PROMOTING SPIRITUAL GROWTH

- **You will need:** a white tea-light (in a jar, if you are outdoors), a rainbow moonstone (a pendant or ring is ideal, available on the Internet).

- **Light the tea-light** before you begin the ritual.

- **Ask the Archangel Gabriel** to empower and oversee the process.

- **Hold the moonstone** in your feminine, intuitive left hand.

- **Sit in a comfortable meditation posture.** Breathe slowly and gently and relax.

- **Imagine, feel, or visualize** that you are breathing in the energies of the moon. Feel your body filling with the moon's light.

- **Breathe this energy into your moonstone** when your intuition tells you to.

- **Hold the moonstone to your heart chakra** and ask Archangel Gabriel to empower it with his magical energy. Then move it to your third-eye chakra and ask for Gabriel's blessings and protection.

- **Wear, carry, or sleep with the moonstone** on a daily basis to increase your spiritual growth.

- **Write down what you experienced** in the space overleaf

My spiritual-growth experience

Date _____ Time _____

I saw _____
_____
_____
_____
_____
_____

I felt _____
_____
_____
_____
_____
_____

I learned _____
_____
_____
_____
_____
_____

My spiritual-growth experience

Date _____ **Time** _____

I saw _____

_____

_____

_____

_____

_____

I felt _____

_____

_____

_____

_____

I learned _____

_____

_____

_____

_____

_____

Meditation for assistance

In this meditation you will be calling on the Archangel Seraphiel of the Seraphim. The Seraphim are a collective of angels bound in one-consciousness (unity of angels), whose mission is to aid humanity by increasing conscious awareness of the Divine. The Seraphim are among the most radiant of all angelic beings and are the closest to God. Archangel Seraphiel has the power and authority to create harmony, balance, and alignment by dynamically clearing built-up stagnant energy around people, situations, and places. He has the ability to modify all blocked conditions.

As always beforehand, make sure that you will not be disturbed: close the door, switch off your phone, dim the lights, burn a little incense, if you wish, or light a candle and place it on your altar, then sit quietly and take a few moments to ground and center yourself in the present moment. These are simple rituals to relax yourself and bring your focus to a meditative state.

Exercise 25 MEDITATION FOR ANGELIC ASSISTANCE

- **Sit on a cushion or chair** in your meditation space.

- **Close your eyes** and relax your body by focusing on your breathing, letting it become slower and deeper, with the out-breath being slower than the in-breath.

- **Allow your aura to expand** to fill the space around you.

- **Summon Archangel Seraphiel** by intoning his name three times: "Seraphiel, Seraphiel, Seraphiel."

- **See, feel, visualize, or know** that you are now surrounded by the most radiant light-being you can imagine.

- **Mentally state whatever you need assistance with,** letting your consciousness merge in a bright sphere of light with the angels.

- **Give thanks to Archangel Seraphiel and the Seraphim** at the end of the ceremony, and send out a worldwide blessing from your heart chakra.

- **Write down what you experienced** in the space overleaf.

My angelic-assistance meditation

Date _____   Time _____

I saw _____

_____

_____

_____

_____

_____

I felt _____

_____

_____

_____

_____

I learned _____

_____

_____

_____

_____

_____

My angelic-assistance meditation

Date _____ **Time** _____

I saw _____

_____

_____

_____

_____

_____

I felt _____

_____

_____

_____

_____

_____

I learned _____

_____

_____

_____

_____

_____

_____

Summoning Archangel Muriel

Call on Archangel Muriel whenever you feel emotionally overwhelmed and are struggling to think clearly and rationally. She will help you to put your troubled feelings into perspective, and will bring you comfort and restore your emotions to a balanced state. This meditation will help you in times of trouble.

Exercise 26 IN TIMES OF TROUBLE MEDITATION

- **Sit in a comfortable meditation posture,** letting the chair beneath you take the full weight of your body, and relax.

- **Allow your eyes to close.**

- **Focus on your breathing,** slowing it down so that the out-breath is slower than the in-breath. Let all tension flow out of your body. Let yourself be lulled into a peaceful state.

- **Summon Archangel Muriel** by saying "Archangel Muriel, please be with me now in my time of need." See, feel, visualize, or know that she is with you, surrounding you with her radiant light and love. Thank her for hearing your prayer.

- **Tell her why you need her help,** either speaking out loud or silently in your thoughts. Now say "Archangel Muriel, please help me to become calm and centered so that I can view this situation in its true light. Guide me so that I act in the ways that are most appropriate and are for the highest good of everyone concerned.'

- **Feel yourself being wrapped in a radiant aquamarine light.** Be receptive to any emotions, images, physical sensations, or thoughts that come to you.

- **When you are ready, give thanks to Archangel Muriel** for being with you. Take three deep breaths, and with each out-breath become more aware of your surroundings. Feel yourself returning to your chair and to the room.

- **Write down what you experienced** and the guidance you received, in the space overleaf.

My in times of trouble meditation experience

Date _____ Time _____

I saw _____
_____
_____
_____
_____
_____
_____

I felt _____
_____
_____
_____
_____
_____

I learned _____
_____
_____
_____
_____
_____
_____

Earth angels group meditation

Here is a guided meditation to use at the start of each gathering of Earth angels. It will help to strengthen the connections between you and create a strong and loving link with the angels that are working with you all.

Exercise 27 EARTH ANGELS GROUP MEDITATION

- **Sit in a circle,** with your feet on the floor. Relax your breathing and ground yourselves (see page 34).

- **Say together,** "Dear angels, we ask that you draw closer to us so that we can sense your presence." Know that they are standing behind you, forming a large circle. Feel the love and protection they are sending you.

- **Say together,** "Dear angels, please bless and protect our Earth angel group, so that we may work today with unconditional love, and so that our work is carried out for the highest good of everyone concerned. Help us to receive the insights and guidance that you send us."

- **Now begin your work as a group.** At the end of your session say, "Thank you, angels, for working with us today. Thank you for the loving support you give our group."

- **Take three deep breaths** and slowly let yourselves come back into the room.

- **Write down what you experienced** in the space overleaf.

My Earth angels group meditation experience

Date _____ **Time** _____

I saw _____
_____
_____
_____
_____
_____
_____

I felt _____
_____
_____
_____
_____
_____

I learned _____
_____
_____
_____
_____
_____
_____

TAKING ANGEL
WORK FURTHER

Developing wisdom

Archangel Jophiel, whose name means "Beauty of God," rules the yellow ray of wisdom and illumination. This influences the solar-plexus chakra, which is why his ray is often called the "sunshine" ray. Jophiel, who is the angel of wisdom, works with the angels from the Halls of Wisdom to bring logical thinking, the attainment of goals, and self-confidence. With his assistance, you can rediscover your enjoyment of life and your sense of fun. He also helps you to connect with your higher self.

In the Kabalistic system, Jophiel rules over the *sephirah* of Hod, in conjunction with the Archangel Michael. Hod represents glory and majesty. Jophiel's gifts include the wisdom flame, intuition, perception, joy, bliss, and soul-illumination.

Invoke Archangel Jophiel whenever you want to boost your creativity, combat lethargy or confusion, or overcome loss of self-esteem. Invoke his wisdom flame when you wish to understand a situation more clearly. Ask Jophiel to help you learn new information or to remember something important.

Physical associations Jophiel boosts, strengthens, tones, and reinforces your energy and your physical body; detoxifies and breaks down fatty deposits and cellulite.

Emotional and mental associations Jophiel enhances your mental abilities and stimulates the intellect; boosts concentration; brings self-confidence; fosters happiness and laughter; and encourages a sense of well-being

Spiritual associations Jophiel boosts your connection with your higher self, your guides and angels; creates links between the spiritual and material worlds; and enables soul-illumination.

Ritual Sit in front of your altar and center yourself. Light a yellow candle and visualize a vortex of golden-yellow light descending around you and forming a sphere of golden light. Absorb this light into every level of your body, mind, and spirit. Use the following affirmation: "Archangel Jophiel, charge my being with spiritual light to bring clarity and wisdom."

 **Work with your angels now** Turn to Exercise 28: Asking for Wisdom Meditation on pages 226–227 to meet Archangel Jophiel

Inspiration

Archangel Gabriel rules the orange ray, which influences the sacral chakra. He is one of the four great archangels. He and Archangel Michael are the only two angels whose names appear in the New Testament. It was Gabriel who, at the Annunciation, told Mary that she would give birth to Jesus. Although he was not named, Gabriel also watched over Jesus' tomb after his crucifixion and told his disciples of his resurrection. In Islam, where he is known as Jibril, he awakened Mohammed, the Prophet of God, and dictated the Koran to him. Gabriel's focus is creativity and the dissolution of fear. His element is water, and his balanced expression is vitality and originality.

In the Kabalistic system, he rules over the *sephirah* of Yesod, the foundation. The literal translation of Gabriel's name is "strong one of God."

Invoke Archangel Gabriel when your inspiration needs a boost, or when you feel blocked. Gabriel will transform fear, guiding you through change. His energy signature is intense, joyful, and optimistic.

Physical associations Gabriel is motivational and revitalizing; he balances the body's energy levels; is beneficial for the lower back, kidneys, and digestive processes; balances the hormones; and aids fertility.

Emotional and mental associations Gabriel eases grief and loss; boosts optimism and a positive approach to life; encourages creativity and inspiration; and soothes fears and phobias.

Spiritual associations Gabriel stimulates joy and is spiritually uplifting and purifying; he is the "messenger" and can help to access your inner angel (angelic nature).

Ritual Sit in front of your altar and center yourself by focusing on your breathing. Light a white candle and visualize a vortex of white light descending around you and forming a sphere of white light. Absorb the light into all levels of your body, mind, and spirit. Use the following affirmation: "Archangel Gabriel, purify my body, mind, and spirit, and awaken my inner angel."

> **Work with your angels now** Turn to Exercise 29: Asking for Guidance
Meditation on pages 230–231 to meet Archangel Gabriel.

Protection and cutting ties

Archangel Michael, whose name means "who can stand against God," is the leader of the archangels. His role is to protect humanity and to lead his "legions of light" in their battle against evil forces, and he is often depicted slaying a dragon. Although he is connected with the fiery power of the solar-plexus chakra, his flaming sapphire sword also links him with the blue ray of the throat chakra.

In the Kabalistic system, he rules over the *sephirah* of Hod in tandem with Archangel Jophiel. Hod represents glory and majesty.

Invoke Archangel Michael to help you release negative energy, gain instant protection, and cut binding ties with other people.

Physical associations Michael's blue ray has a soothing effect on all conditions associated with heat and inflammation; and helps to calm the central nervous system, reducing tension and anxiety.

Emotional and mental associations
Michael has a calming impact on all mental processes, encouraging clarity of thought; creates a peaceful detachment from worldly problems; and encourages the ability to speak the truth.

Spiritual associations Michael inspires the search for higher truths and hidden knowledge; his blue ray encourages the surrender of the little will (the ego) to the higher will of God; and protects against the shadow of illusion.

Ritual Sit in front of your altar and center yourself by focusing on your breathing. Light a blue candle and visualize a vortex of sapphire-blue light descending around you and forming a sphere of blue light. Absorb the light into all levels of your body, mind, and spirit. Ask Archangel Michael to wrap his blue cloak of protection around you. Use the following affirmation: "Archangel Michael, protect me, cut all cords that bind me to this situation."

 Work with your angels now Turn to Exercise 30: Asking for Protection Meditation on pages 234–235 to meet Archangel Michael.

Spiritual growth

Archangel Zadkiel, whose name means "the righteousness of God," is the angel of mercy. Also known as "the holy one," he teaches trust in God's benevolence and brings you comfort whenever you need it. He was the angel who prevented Abraham from sacrificing his son, Isaac, on Mount Moriah. Zadkiel is one of the seven great angels that stand before the throne of God. He rules over the crown chakra, corresponding to the violet ray. His violet flame focuses on self-transformation, spiritual growth, and cosmic alchemy.

In the Kabalistic system, Zadkiel rules over the *sephirah* of Chesed, which represents mercy.

Invoke Archangel Zadkiel when you need to release your judgmental thoughts or seek spiritual transformation. Call on him if your past prevents you from manifesting your dreams.

Physical associations Zadkiel assists the correct functioning of the immune system and aids the healing process; reduces swellings, bruises, and eye strain.

Emotional and mental associations
Zadkiel calms and removes emotional turbulence; and ameliorates addictions and addictive traits within the personality.

Spiritual associations Zadkiel boosts inspiration, imagination, intuition, and psychic abilities, making it easier to see visions; encourages spiritual dedication and evokes significant dreams; aids meditation and past-life regression; helps you to develop to the crown chakra and gain access to the higher mind; and provides psychic protection; Zadkiel's violet flame purifies everything it touches, making it a powerful healer of the mind and body.

Ritual Stand in front of your altar and center yourself by focusing on your breathing. Light a violet candle and visualize a vortex of violet light descending around you and forming a violet flame. Feel the light purifying your body, mind, and spirit. Use the following affirmation: "Archangel Zadkiel, direct the violet flame of freedom into all areas of my body, chakras, and aura, until I am purified of all negativity."

Finding love

Archangel Chamuel rules over the element of air and the pink ray—a balanced union of Heaven and Earth within the human heart, resulting from the alchemical combination of the physical red ray with the white ray of spiritual awakening. Chamuel works through the heart chakra and the pink ray to renew and improve your loving relationships. He increases your ability to love others and to receive love from them unconditionally, without any thought of gain or merit. It is a form of love that is transcendent, transformational, and compassionate, helping you to move closer toward enlightenment.

In the Kabalistic system, Chamuel rules over the *sephirah* of Geburah or severity.

Invoke Archangel Chamuel to cleanse and balance your heart chakra.

Physical associations Chamuel heals any part of the body that you dislike; soothes physical tension; and combats the fear of illness that can prevent you from healing.

Emotional and mental associations Chamuel dissolves self-loathing, selfishness, and depression; and encourages a belief in your unique talents.

Spiritual associations Chamuel opens the heart and attracts soulmates; and prepares you to receive the Christ-consciousness, the Holy Spirit.

Ritual Sit on a cushion and focus your mind on your heart chakra. Place your left palm in the center of your chest and your right hand on top of your left. Close your eyes. Visualize your heart chakra's 12 lotus petals. As you view them, notice whether any are damaged —some may even be closed. Ask the Archangel Chamuel to open the petals and repair any damaged ones. The normal color of the heart lotus petals is green, but as you evolve spiritually they change to a beautiful shade of pink; see how many of your heart petals are now pink. Repeat this process until all your heart-chakra petals are healthy and pink. Use the following affirmation: "Archangel Chamuel, heal my heart, help me attract a soulmate."

Assistance on your life path

The ruby ray of the Archangel Uriel influences the root chakra. In the Kabalistic system, Uriel rules over the *sephirah* of Malkuth, or the kingdom.

Invoke Archangel Uriel whenever you feel lost, fearful, forsaken, rejected, or suicidal. If you are not happy with your work or are unsure of your life path, Uriel will show you the way.

Physical associations Uriel teaches you to listen to the wisdom of your body.

Emotional and mental associations Uriel represents brilliant ideas and creative insights.

Spiritual associations Uriel stands for spiritual devotion through selfless service to others.

Ritual Sit in front of your altar. Contemplate your life as you light a red candle and visualize a vortex of ruby-red light forming a sphere around you. Absorb the light of God into all levels of your body, mind, and spirit. Ask Archangel Uriel to illuminate your life path. Use the following affirmation: "Archangel Uriel, bring peace to my mind and spirit. Dissolve all obstacles on my spiritual path by showing me my true path in this life so that I can fulfill my destiny."

 ➤ **Work with your angels now** Turn to Exercise 31: Asking for Renewed Energy Meditation on pages 238–239 to meet Archangel Uriel

Divination

Angels can also assist you to look into the future. One popular way to seek angelic assistance in the art of prophecy is through cloud formations. Traditionally people perceived angels as flying between Heaven and Earth, and so naturally the sky is their domain. Indeed, many people have seen angelic forms in the clouds in times of great personal need. Meditating on cloud formations (aeromancy) can be a good way of tuning into angelic vibrations. Simply sit down and gaze at the sky from a good vantage point—a hill or the window of a high building will do, but the best results come from when you lie flat on your back gazing up at the sky. As you lie, weightless and relaxed, tune into the shifting patterns, and detect wings or even the image of a complete angel.

Case study
A presence in the clouds
I was coming back from the hospital where I'd been visiting my grandmother who was very ill. I was distressed to see her so helpless. My shoulders were hunched over with worry, my head bent, eyes on the ground, but some instinct made me look up to the sky. At that moment the most extraordinary cloud formation appeared on the horizon: it looked like a giant hand reaching down protectively toward me. Instantly I felt comforted and reassured, able to deal with whatever came next.

 Work with your angels now Turn to Exercise 32: Cloud Divination on page 241, to perform your own cloud divination.

 I'm not quite there yet If you're having trouble seeing patterns in the clouds, try Exercise 9: Your Angel Vision on page 98 again, freely using the paint to record the formations you see in the sky. Is any shape starting to emerge on your paper?

Angel cards

One excellent way to communicate with your guardian angel, as well as with other spirit guides, is to use a set of angel cards. You can buy a set from a New Age bookshop or on the Internet. Usually each card bears a single word of encouragement or a short, reassuring phrase that helps you focus on a particular aspect of your inner life.

These commercially available cards can be useful, but it is much more effective to create your own set of angel cards. You can make them as decorative or as plain as you wish, according to your taste and your artistic talents. For very simple cards, all you need is a pen and some stiff paper or card (which, ideally, should be colored on one side and white on the other). If you wish, you can stick some small, shiny angel shapes on the cards, which dedicates them to the angels. On the white side of each card write a positive quality—called a keyword—that you would like to bring into your life. There is no end to the number of positive qualities associated

with angels, and you can always add to your set of cards as new keywords occur to you.

How to use your angel cards
There are many different ways of working with your angel cards:
* Select a card at random at the start of each day: spend a few moments thinking about the day ahead, then fan out the cards (with their white sides away from you) and see which one attracts your attention. Keep that card with you, or place it where you will be able to see it throughout the day.
* Choose a card before you begin a new venture or project, and on your birthday to give you insight into the coming year.
* Choose an angel card to help a friend with a problem. Mentally surround your friend with the angelic quality of the card in question.
* At the start of the new year, select one card for each of the coming 12 months. Make a note of each card on your calendar or in your diary.

EXERCISES TO
TAKE ANGEL WORK
FURTHER

These exercises will deepen your understanding
of the angelic realm.

Asking Archangel Jophiel for wisdom

Archangel Jophiel is the angel to call on when you need to benefit from his wisdom. Ask him to help you when your thoughts are fragmented and it is difficult to think logically and coherently. He is especially helpful if you want to understand difficult problems and gain deep insight into your life, or if you want to know how to proceed with a troubling situation.

Exercise 28 ASKING FOR WISDOM MEDITATION

- **Sit in a comfortable meditation posture,** letting the chair beneath you take the full weight of your body, and relax.

- **Allow your eyes to close.**

- **Focus on your breathing,** slowing it down so that the out-breath is slower than the in-breath. Let all tension flow out of your body. Let your mind grow quiet and still.

- **Ask to be taken to Archangel Jophiel's ashram** above Lanchow in China. Feel yourself being transported there. Notice any changes in the energy around you.

- **Summon Archangel Jophiel** by saying, "Archangel Jophiel, please come to me now so that I can benefit from your Divine wisdom and guidance." See, feel, visualize, or know that he is with you, surrounding you with his radiant yellow light. Thank him for hearing your prayer.

- **Tell Archangel Jophiel why you need his help,** either speaking out loud or silently in your thoughts.

- **Feel yourself being wrapped in the yellow light of his wisdom.** Allow your consciousness to merge with his. Be receptive to any emotions, images, physical sensations, or thoughts that come to you.

- **When you are ready,** give thanks to Archangel Jophiel for being with you. Take three deep breaths, and with each out-breath become more aware of your surroundings. Feel yourself returning to your chair and to the room.

- **Write down what you experienced** and the guidance you received, in the space overleaf.

My asking for wisdom meditation experience

Date _____ **Time** _____

I saw _____

_____

_____

_____

_____

_____

I felt _____

_____

_____

_____

_____

_____

I learned _____

_____

_____

_____

_____

_____

My asking for wisdom meditation experience

Date _____ Time _____

I saw _____
_____
_____
_____
_____
_____

I felt _____
_____
_____
_____
_____
_____

I learned _____
_____
_____
_____
_____
_____
_____

Asking Archangel Gabriel for guidance

Archangel Gabriel is the angel to call on when you need guidance about making major changes to your life, if you are thinking of embarking on a new project, or when you feel your life has reached a turning point. You can ask him to dissolve any fears you are experiencing about the changes taking place in your life.

Exercise 29 ASKING FOR GUIDANCE MEDITATION

- **Sit in a comfortable meditation posture,** letting the chair beneath you take the full weight of your body, and relax.

- **Allow your eyes to close.**

- **Focus on your breathing,** slowing it down so that the out-breath is slower than the in-breath. Let all tension flow out of your body. Let your mind grow quiet and still.

- **Ask to be taken to Archangel Gabriel's ashram** above Mount Shasta in California. Feel yourself being transported there. Notice any changes in the energy around you.

- **Summon Archangel Gabriel** by saying, "Archangel Gabriel, please come to me now so that you can guide me and help me to choose the right path." See, feel, visualize, or know that he is with you, surrounding you with his shining white light. Thank him for hearing your prayer.

- **Tell him why you need his assistance,** either speaking out loud or silently in your thoughts. Ask him to bring into your life the people and circumstances that will help you to succeed in your plans.

- **Feel yourself being wrapped in the radiant white light of his guidance.** Allow your consciousness to merge with his. Be receptive to any emotions, images, physical sensations, or thoughts that come to you.

- **When you are ready,** give thanks to Archangel Gabriel for being with you. Take three deep breaths, and with each out-breath become more aware of your surroundings. Feel yourself returning to your chair and to the room.

- **Write down what you experienced** and the guidance you received, in the space overleaf.

My asking for guidance meditation experience

Date _____ Time _____

I saw _____
_____
_____
_____
_____
_____

I felt _____
_____
_____
_____
_____
_____

I learned _____
_____
_____
_____
_____
_____
_____

My asking for guidance meditation experience

Date _____ Time _____

I saw _____
_____
_____
_____
_____
_____

I felt _____
_____
_____
_____
_____

I learned _____
_____
_____
_____
_____
_____

Asking Archangel Michael for protection

Archangel Michael is the angel to call on when you are in need of immediate protection and strength. Michael will protect your belongings as well as your physical body. You can also ask Michael to help you to release any fears and obsessions that are holding you back.

Exercise 30 ASKING FOR PROTECTION MEDITATION

- **Sit in a comfortable meditation posture,** letting the chair beneath you take the full weight of your body, and relax.

- **Allow your eyes to close.**

- **Focus on your breathing,** slowing it down so that the out-breath is slower than the in-breath. Let all tension flow out of your body. Let your mind grow quiet and still.

- **Ask to be taken to Archangel Michael's ashram** above the Paradise Valley in Canada. Feel yourself being transported there. Notice any changes in the energy around you.

- **Summon Archangel Michael** by saying, "Archangel Michael, please come to me now so that I can benefit from your immediate protection. Help me to feel safe and secure, confident that you are protecting me from all ills." See, feel, visualize, or know that he is with you, surrounding you with his brilliant sapphire-blue light. Thank him for hearing your prayer.

- **Tell him why you need his help,** either speaking out loud or silently in your thoughts. Ask him to dissolve your fears, to remove your phobias, and to strengthen your faith in God.

- **Feel yourself being wrapped in the vibrant blue light of his protection.** Allow your consciousness to merge with his. Be receptive to any emotions, images, physical sensations, or thoughts that come to you.

- **When you are ready,** give thanks to Archangel Michael for being with you. Take three deep breaths, and with each out-breath become more aware of your surroundings. Feel yourself returning to your chair and to the room.

- **Write down what you experienced** and the guidance you received, in the space overleaf.

My asking for protection meditation experience

Date _____ **Time** _____

I saw _____
_____
_____
_____
_____
_____

I felt _____
_____
_____
_____
_____
_____

I learned _____
_____
_____
_____
_____
_____
_____

My asking for protection meditation experience

Date _____ **Time** _____

I saw _____
_____
_____
_____
_____
_____

I felt _____
_____
_____
_____
_____

I learned _____
_____
_____
_____
_____
_____

Asking Archangel Uriel for renewed energy

Archangel Uriel is the angel to summon when you feel you have lost your way through life and you want to be put back on the right path. He will help you to know your own mind, to find the right direction, and to discover a renewed purpose in life. You should call on Uriel when you are depressed, feel suicidal, are lacking in energy or recovering from illness.

Exercise 31 ASKING FOR RENEWED ENERGY MEDITATION

- **Sit in a comfortable meditation posture,** letting the chair beneath you take the full weight of your body, and relax.

- **Allow your eyes to close.**

- **Focus on your breathing,** slowing it down so that the out-breath is slower than the in-breath. Let all tension flow out of your body. Let your mind grow quiet and still.

- **Ask to be taken to Archangel Uriel's ashram** above the Tatra Mountains in Poland. Feel yourself being transported there. Notice any changes in the energy around you.

- **Summon Archangel Uriel** by saying, "Archangel Uriel, please come to me now so that you can boost my energy levels. Be at my side so that I may strengthen my resolve. Illuminate the path that I tread through life so that I may find my way again. Support me when I stumble, take my hand when I falter, and give me the courage to continue." See, feel, visualize, or know that he is with you, surrounding you with his rich ruby light. Thank him for hearing your prayer.

- **Tell him why you need his assistance,** either speaking out loud or silently in your thoughts. Ask him to give you his steadfast support.

- **Feel yourself being wrapped in the deep ruby light of his guidance.** Allow your consciousness to merge with his. Be receptive to any emotions, images, physical sensations, or thoughts that come to you.

- **When you are ready,** give thanks to Archangel Uriel for being with you. Take three deep breaths, and with each out-breath become more aware of your surroundings. Feel yourself returning to your chair and to the room.

- **Write down what you experienced,** and the guidance you received, in the space overleaf.

My asking for renewed energy meditation experience

Date _____ **Time** _____

I saw _____

_____

_____

_____

_____

_____

I felt _____

_____

_____

_____

_____

_____

I learned _____

_____

_____

_____

_____

_____

_____

Cloud divination

Angels often have messages for us, although they may not be delivered in an obvious way. It is up to you to develop your sensitivity and responsiveness. Sometimes messages are provided in the form of cloud patterns—particular shapes will emerge that relate to issues that currently concern you.

Depending on the time of year and prevailing weather, particular angels are more likely to be in attendance, and you may wish to direct your attention to a specific archangel if you are seeking guidance. For example, the Archangel Michael governs the south and bestows protection.

Exercise 32 CLOUD DIVINATION

- Visit a local park or garden where you are free to lie down on the ground undisturbed and at peace.

- Tune into your breathing and let your eyes close when you feel fully relaxed.

- Open your eyes and gaze up at the clouds above you. Don't focus too hard Let the clouds drift in and out of your vision.

- Write down what you saw in the clouds in the space overleaf, and what you learned from the experience.

My cloud-divination experience

Date _____ **Time** _____

I saw _____
_____
_____
_____
_____
_____
_____

I felt _____
_____
_____
_____
_____
_____

I learned _____
_____
_____
_____
_____
_____
_____

REAL-LIFE
EXPERIENCES

An angelic vision

The angelic realm is all around us, at all times. We only have to "raise our vibrational awareness" to become aware that we dance in the waves of Divine creation. The vastness of this glory is ours to see, if we attune our senses. The following story is a prime example of what can happen when we dissolve the dream of delusion and view ourselves as part of this changeless Divine Being.

Case study
Angel seminar

Toward the end of the second day of an archangel-enlightenment course in beautiful Bournemouth we were chanting the Om mantra when several bright lights appeared in the corner of the room. Everyone present saw them and, as we gazed at them, they gently moved to and fro. Suddenly a beautiful angelic face, haloed in light and framed by a pair of vast pure-white wings, was clearly visible. It was one of the most profound group experiences. Some of those present were overwhelmed by this unforgettable, unfolding spectacle. All participants felt a deep sense of perfect peace and joy, and the healing vibrations were clearly tangible.

The Om mantra is the sound of creation and means "peace." It enables us to feel in every cell of our body the Divine joy and peace of meditation.

The spirit of obsidian

I personally have the crystal obsidian as one of my "spirit" guides. The spirit of obsidian chose me—not the other way around. As we work with crystals, some of them become very special to us. They choose to act as a personal totem energy or ally. A totem energy is completely reliable in all situations and acts as a guide on all levels, very much like a personal guardian angel.

Case study
Obsidian goddess-angel

In the late summer of 1990 I was teaching a crystal course in Manchester; it was the first weekend of this particular course, so I had not met all the students. The night before I had a dream in which a beautiful goddess-angel appeared; she was dressed in flowing, iridescent, sparkling clothes and wore a headdress of feathers interwoven with shimmering jewels. As she stood before me, she held out her hand: on it were three very long, strange-looking claws like crystal blades; they were curved, dark, translucent, and exotic-looking. She said, "Choose one." As I gazed at them in wonder I asked, "What are they?" She replied, "Crows' claws." In the shamanic tradition, crow medicine represents Truth, Wise Counsel, Wisdom, and Resourcefulness. I then chose a "claw."

The next day, during the lunchtime break, one of the students approached me; she looked very shy, hesitant, and a little perplexed. She said, "Yesterday I was in a crystal shop in London and I was looking at these. I have never seen anything like them before. I was told by my angel guide to buy three; one is yours." As she stood before me she held out her hand; on it were three very long, exotic-looking, claw-like crystal blades; they were curved, dark, translucent, and strange-looking. She said, "Choose one." Yes, you have guessed it: they were a type of natural obsidian blade that I had never seen before. Yes, I was chosen by the obsidian. I have used the "claws" continually in my healing work.

Angelic signature

As a child, I saw beautiful angels in my bedroom every night. These were the most exquisite creatures you could imagine—they "gifted" to me a serenity and deep sense of peace. I was frequently comforted by them throughout my difficult childhood. I know I am not alone in this childhood experience, because one of my students shared her first angelic encounter with me. I felt honored that she chose to share it with me, for I know she had never told anyone before.

Case study
Archangel Michael

Her encounter happened when she was nine years old and was going through a very bad time at home. Her early life had been difficult, to say the least, and one night as she lay in her bed, she said that the ceiling dissolved and she saw before her the most exquisite angel carrying a sword of pure-blue flame. The sense of perfect protection and guidance from this beautiful being changed her young life, and she has now been able to grow into adulthood whole and healthy, despite many negative family situations.

The amazing thing is that I knew she had experienced an encounter with the Archangel Michael even before she told me, because she carried his angelic signature within her energy field. I noticed it the first moment she walked into the room—I could feel it, we smiled and instantly angelic recognition passed between us.

Sacred sound

Sound therapy plays a profound, intricate, and fundamental role in my angel seminars and healing practice.

Case study
Archangel Shamael

I often use group mantras and chanting, but on one occasion I was using my favorite clear-quartz singing bowl, which is harmonically tuned to the crown chakra note of B, and one of the angel essences that I have personally created, dedicated to the Archangel Shamael (the angel of sacred sound), to purify and harmonize the energy field of a workshop participant. I must add here that I had never met this lady before and had no idea of her current medical history—this was simply a demonstration exercise.

The lady was gently helped to lie down on a therapy couch by one of my regular crystal students. I began sounding the crystal bowl around her. Suddenly she was laughing and crying tears of joy as she finally explained that she could now feel her feet! Her serious medical condition meant that she had lost most of the sensations in her feet and lower legs. All the angel-seminar participants were overjoyed at such a wonderful experience. Of course the lady became a regular client of mine, and we continued with these angelic-sound sessions, which seemed greatly to assist her.

Angel attunement

In the 1990s I ran a series of one-day experiential workshops to assist people to acquire a greater awareness of the angelic realm. I was guided by the angels to offer an "angel attunement," which was very much like a "Reiki attunement" (I have been a Mikao Usui Shiki Ryoho Reiki Master and Tibetan Master since 1994 and a Karuna Master since 1995). I used an ancient "angelic" symbol that the angels had given me as a child; this symbol is used to activate the crown, heart, and hand chakras. The people I attuned to this angelic energy were then able to pass "angelic-healing" energy on to others and could incorporate this energy into their own healing practice.

Case study
Angel symbol

On one occasion one of the workshop participants had an unexpected "healing" experience, when he felt an amazing amount of energy coursing through his system at the attunement, and was on "cloud nine" for most of the day afterward. But it was only after the attunement that the "healing" fully manifested itself, for he found that he no longer had any desire or craving to smoke cigarettes ever again. He is still smoke-free. The ancient angelic symbol I was given for attuning others to the angelic realm is the "winged heart," which—when used consciously with love—instantly raises the vibratory signature of the room and the energy resonance there.

Angels' blessing

One weekend I was in Bournemouth for my crystal course. The weather was glorious as usual. The group was in high spirits, because it was the final weekend of their two-year professional crystal-therapy course. They were in graduation mood!

Case study
Graduation

During the opening session (which I call "checking in"), when we share what has been happening in our lives since we were last together, I decided for my part to share and demonstrate a new angel essence that I had produced since our last session in May. One of the ladies in the group became totally transfixed and transported. She seemed to be in another world, another dimension. She was gazing past and above me. This lasted for several minutes. When finally she was able to speak, she described what she had witnessed. I was totally surrounded by angels, and one in particular was "overshadowing" me and channeling a beautiful stream of energy toward me and the angel essence that I was demonstrating. This healing energy flooded outward to the crystal group and then streamed out into Bournemouth. This could explain something that has always puzzled my groups: we always get the most beautiful weather— even in the dead of winter; perhaps this is the angels' blessing on my groups, or perhaps the angels know that I used to live in Spain and miss the sunshine. Either way, everyone wins by this blessing.

Web of light

A crystal can only be called a "power" stone when it manifests in all the chakra or rainbow colors. There are several crystals that manifest this amazing spectrum of hues. Under this definition, calcite, tourmaline, and sapphire are "power" stones.

Case study

Ayurveda (Sanskrit word for "science of life")

A student of mine was demonstrating a crystal web of light that she had designed as part of the crystal course. She was using the "power" stone, calcite. The student needed a partner (client) to demonstrate on, and a volunteer was quickly found and the therapy session began. As each colored calcite stone was laid on the relevant chakra, the energy of the room became very still and peaceful. Angels appeared and surrounded the student and client with beautiful, fluid-cleansing energy. I was not the only one watching this energy as it unfolded. The "client" said afterward, "It was as if water was being poured over my third-eye chakra" (this energy center is also known as the "Christ-consciousness center").

This is exactly what I and several of the students perceived and testified to. It was as if an ancient Ayurvedic technique called Shirodhara was being conducted by an angel. In Shirodhara warm oil is poured over the forehead, which calms and pacifies the central nervous system, enabling stress to be released. So long as we dwell on the material plane, human consciousness cannot encompass the universal energy that we often refer to as "Christ-consciousness." By practicing meditation and refining our consciousness, we can ultimately perceive the "Christ-consciousness" that is universally present in all creation.

A sign from a guardian angel

This final story comes from Fiona Murray, the author of *Messages from Nature's Guardians*, who sells my angel essences at her own angel seminars.

Case study
Feathers

I started hearing angels four years ago. They told me that I was to become a spiritual author working with nature angels, but also that they wanted me to do introductory talks on guardian angels. An opportunity came up at a local hotel to do weekly after-dinner speeches, so I started to teach people. Sometimes the audiences were keen to learn, while on other occasions they were more skeptical.

One time, with an audience of 40 people, I had just finished saying that angels give us signs all the time, especially by leaving white feathers, which appear as if from nowhere. The room we were meeting in had a high, pyramidal glass roof. One lady found a feather "descending from the sky" as she put it, and it fell onto her lap. As she stood up to show me, the audience gasped. I smiled and told her that the guardian angels wanted her to know how loved she was, and that she wasn't alone. For the following few weeks the same thing kept happening among the audiences.

Now, before I start my talks, I silently ask the angels to give the people in the audience whatever sign it is that they require to help them start to connect with their guardian angels. Feathers are definitely the favored choice by the angelic realm, and at every angel talk now one appears.

Index

A

Adam and Eve 25, 86
affirmations 92, 194–5
air spirits 32
Akashic Records 25
alignment 78–80
altars 84–5, 100–1
angel-aura quartz 63,
    175
angelic humans 190
angelic signature 246
angelite 59, 61
apophyllite 62
appearance of angels
    90
Aquinas, St Thomas 88
Archangel Enlightenment
    188
archangels 8, 9, 16, 26
    meditation on 46–9
Ariel 28
Ascended Masters
    190
ashrams 16, 94–6
attunement 248
auras 16, 43, 61
Auriel 30, 61, 184
azeztulite 59

B

base chakra 52, 66
blessings 249
    altars 100–1
blue anhydrite 61
brow chakra 67

C

Camael 25, 30, 123, 126
cards, angel 224
celestite 34, 59, 60
Celtic angels 118, 138–9
chakras 16, 50–7, 61, 62
    angelic-chakra activation
        57, 59, 70–3
    awareness visualization
        57, 66–9, 151
    yoga poses and 52–7
Chamuel 25, 28, 62, 96,
    103, 108
    finding love 218
    healing 150, 151, 164–5
Cherubim 22
Chiron 124
Christianity 18, 26, 118, 212
clairvoyance 186
cloud divination 222,
    240–2

colors
    chakras 51
    healing 154, 156, 162
    temples of light 96
crown chakra 50, 51, 61,
    67
    yoga pose 56
crystals 34, 42, 58–64,
    250
    angelic alignment
        78–80
    cleansing 74
    dream healing 175
    meditation 74–5
    obsidian 245

D

danburite 60
demons 25
destiny 184
devas 32
distant healing 154–5
divination 222, 240–2
Dominations (Dominions)
    25
dream healing 156–7,
    175–6
dreaming 60, 62

E

Earth angels 188
  group meditation
    207–8
Earth spirits 32
elemental kingdom 32
emotional assistance 180,
  182
emotional healing 150–1
energies, exploring angel
  38–41, 64
Enoch, Book of 26, 190
etheric realm 16

F

fairies 32
"fallen" angels 18
fire spirits 32
forgiveness 152

G

Gabriel 9, 22, 25, 26, 30,
  212
  chakra 51
  guidance from 230–1
  healing 158
  planet 123
  spiritual growth 196,
    197
  temple of light 96, 109
  tree of life 102
gemstones 59

God and angels 18, 86,
  114, 116, 118
guardian angels 8, 16, 20,
  26, 70, 113–44
  collage 134–7
  contact with 114
  exercises to attract
    129–44
  journey experience
    130–3
  signs from 251
guidance 158, 230–3
guiding angels 116–17

H

Hagiel 123, 126
Haniel 26, 30, 96, 109,
  123, 180
healing meditation 162–3
heart chakra 50, 51, 148,
  197, 218
  awareness visualization
    66
  crystals 62
  yoga pose 54
hierarchies of angels 16, 18,
  22–6
Honorius Augustodunensis
  118

I

inspiration 212

Islam 18, 212

J

Jophiel 22, 28, 51, 96,
  210, 226–7
journal-keeping 11, 12
Jupiter 122, 123, 124

K

the Kabala 86–7, 186,
  210, 216

L

legions of light 16
letters to angels 192
light-workers 16
Lords (Lordships) 25
love, finding 218
loving meditation
  164–7

M

mantras 16, 92, 244
Mars 122, 123, 124
meditation
  archangels 46–9
  assistance 200–3
  crystal 74–5
  Earth angels groups
    207–8
  guardian angels 130–3,
    138–44

guidance 230–3
healing 162–3
loving 164–7
planetary healing 172–4
protection 234–7
renewed energy
    238–40
sound 106–7
spiritual growth 168–9
temples of light 108–12
times of trouble 204–6
tree of life 102–5
wisdom 226–9
Melchizedek 30, 96
Mercury 122, 123, 124
mermaids 32
Metatron 22, 31, 90, 154,
    190
temple 96
tree of life 103
Michael 9, 16, 22, 26,
    30, 188
angelic signature 246
chakra 51
evoking inspiration
    212
planet 123
protection 214, 234–5
temple of light 96,
    108, 109
tree of life 102
moldavite 64

the Moon 122, 123, 124
Muriel 25, 28, 178, 182,
    204–6

N
Nameless Light 59
nature spirits 32
near-death experiences 146
Neptune 122, 123, 125

O
obsidian, spirit of 245

P
physical healing 140–5
planetary healing 172–4
Plato 118
Pluto 122, 123, 125
Powers 25
prayers 88–9, 92, 118
Principalities 26
protection 214, 234–7

R
Raphael 22, 26, 28, 51,
    70
healing 148, 149, 162
planet 123
temple of light 96, 109
tree of life 103
Raziel 22, 31, 51, 86, 186
relationships 160, 164–7

relaxation exercise 34–7
renewed energy 238–40
root chakra 50, 51
rose quartz 42, 62

S
Sabrael 28
sacral chakra 50, 51, 66,
    212
yoga pose 53
salamanders 32
Sandalphon 28, 96, 102,
    154, 190
healing 154, 172–3
Saturn 122, 123, 124
selenite 58, 61
Seraphiel 22, 30, 200
Seraphim 22, 200, 201
seraphinite 64
seriphos green quartz
    63
Shamael 90, 96, 106,
    109, 247
Shirodbara 250
singing bowls 74, 90,
    106, 247
solar plexus chakra 50, 51,
    210
awareness visualization
    66
yoga pose 54
soul-star chakra 61

soulmates 150, 218
sound 90–3, 247
    meditation 106–7
spheres, angels of the 26,
    42–5
spiritual growth 196–9,
    216
spiritual healing 152–3,
    168–9
the Sun 122, 123, 124
Swedenborg, Emanuel
    190
sylphs 32

T
temples of light 16, 94–6
    meditation 108–12
third-eye chakra 35, 50, 51,
    70, 186
    and crystals 61, 62
    yoga pose 56
throat chakra 50, 51, 67
    yoga pose 55
Thrones 22

Thuriel 28
thymus chakra 180
times of trouble meditation
    204–6
tree of life 86, 87, 102–5
the *Trisagion* 22
Tzaphkiel 22, 30, 96, 109
    healing 156, 175

U
Uranus 122, 123, 124
Uriel 25, 26, 30, 51, 96,
    102
    assistance from 220,
        238–9
    healing 160
    planet 123

V
Venus 122, 123, 124
Virgin Mary 22
Virtues 25
visions of angels 82–3,
    98–9, 244

W
water spirits 32
web of light 250
wisdom 210, 226 9

Y
yoga poses 52–7

Z
Zadkiel 22, 25, 30
    chakra 51
    healing 152, 168–9
    planet 123
    spiritual growth 216
    temple of light 96, 109
    tree of life 103
zodiac angels 123, 126–8,
    140–4
Zoroastrianism 118

Acknowledgments

I would like to thank the angelic realm and the grace of God for their love, support, and guidance as I was writing and researching this book and my other angel books. A special thank you to the thousands of people who have attended my angel seminars over the last 19 years and freely shared their experiences, stories and ways of looking at angels. Finally, I would like to thank my family, especially my grandson Gabriel, for their unconditional love and support.

Picture acknowledgments

AKG 19; Cameraphoto 21; Erich Lessing 27. **Alamy** Insadco Photography 179; Mary Evans Picture Library 121; Mary Seton 119; Michelle Chaplow 147; The Art Gallery Collection 191. **Bridgeman Art Library** Museo de Arte de Catalunya, Barcelona, Spain 93; Private Collection/J P Zenobel 127; **Corbis** Araldo de Luca 117; Arte & Immagini srl 29; Blue Lantern Studio 86; John La Farge 32; Jon Arnold 95; Robert Harding World Imagery 94; Trinette Reed/Blend Images 219. **Fotolia** Adroach 1; Matthew Bowden 1. **Getty Images** Botanica 149; Dejan Patic 93; Gary John Norman 151; John Fedele 157; Purestock 189; Tim Robberts 185. **Masterfile** Horst Herget 181. **Octopus Publishing Group** 8, 58, 59, 60, 61, 62, 63, 64, 85, 153, 223; Russell Sadur 2, 9, 10, 13, 15, 89, 91, 155, 159, 213, 215, 221; Ruth Jenkinson 50, 52, 53, 54, 55, 56, 57, 187, 211, 217. **Photolibrary** Larry Williams 183. **Photo Scala, Florence** 24; White Images 31. **Science Photo Library** David Nunuk 125; Lynette Cook 122. **Superstock** 83, 115

Executive Editor: Sandra Rigby

Managing Editor: Clare Churly

Creative Director: Tracy Killick

Designer: Cobalt ID

Assistant Production Controller: Vera Janke